... a Meeting

*Until Stephe... ...eeting, I was always shooting
myself in the f... ...que has cleaned up all that self-destructive
behavior and smoothed the way for making the transition from stand-
up to acting and starring in a series. Now, I can be in a room with the
most powerful people in show business and shine.*

—Christopher Titus (*Titus*)

The Actor Takes a Meeting *is an innovative and exceptional book
about losing one's fear and learning how to take charge of any meeting.
It gave me tremendous insight into the actor's process.*

—Barry Josephson, former President of Columbia Pictures,
Producer (*Men in Black*)

*I applaud another valuable Book book. Stephen gives great advice to
actors about not falling into the victim trap, owning the space, and
finding the right attitude for success.*

—Rick Pagano, Casting Director
(*X-Men: The Last Stand*, "24")

*If you're not getting the representation or acting jobs you deserve, this
is the book for you. Stephen Book illustrates exactly what you've been
doing wrong and how to correct it. As a former agent, manager, and
producer I've taken countless meetings with actors who desperately
needed this advice. He even paints a clear picture of how I've been
reacting to what you've been doing wrong. I had no idea it was that
transparent.*

—Bruce Smith, President, OmniPop Talent Group

*This is a wonderful book—filled with valuable information that
every actor needs in order to participate within the industry without
losing ones sense of self.*

—Peter Levine, Creative Artists Agency

The Actor Takes a Meeting *is a guide to changing the actor's fear into authenticity and presence. This book is a gift to the actor.*
—April Webster, Casting Director
(*Lost, Mission: Impossible III*)

Stephen Book's interview technique is one of the most valuable tools for the actor. It is a "how-to" for making an authentic connection. I vividly remember one of the best general meetings I had: It was easy, fun, and the time just flew by. As we were saying goodbye and I finally glanced at her résumé, I saw that she had indeed studied with Stephen Book. I was not surprised.
—Liz Dean, Casting Director (*Nip/Tuck, Everwood*)

This smart, practical guide to getting what you want gives the actor invaluable tools for climbing the show-biz ladder.
—Gene Parseghian, Parseghian Planco Management

Powerful! Most actors don't even know that they blow it in meetings. Read this book and see what you are doing wrong and how to fix it.
—Tom Parziale, President, Visionary Entertainment

Through reading Book's book and doing the exercises you develop the confidence to own the meeting.
—Bernard Carneol, COO, Progressive Artists Agency

Finally, a guide for any actor who is having difficulty with the all-important meetings that are essential for a successful career. Whether it be feelings of insecurity, victimization, or second-guessing oneself, guidance and exercises can be found in this book to gain confidence and ease the stress in meeting with agents, producers, and casting directors.
—Terry Berland, Commercials Casting Director

This is a revolutionary book. To teach actors how to get what they want through honesty, presence, and self-empowerment is not only bold and daring, but also healthy for the soul.
—Todd Black, Producer (*Pursuit of Happiness, Antoine Fisher*)

THE
ACTOR
TAKES A
MEETING

Also by Stephen Book:

Book on Acting: Improvisation Technique for the Professional Actor in Film, Theater, and Television

THE ACTOR TAKES A MEETING

How to Interview Successfully with Agents, Managers, Producers, and Casting Directors

Stephen Book

SILMAN-JAMES PRESS   LOS ANGELES

First Edition

10 9 8 7 6 5 4 3 2 1

Library of Congress Cataloging-in-Publication Data
Book, Stephen
The actor takes a meeting : how to interview successfully with agents,
managers, producers, and casting directors / by Stephen Book.—1st ed.
p. cm.
Includes bibliographical references.
ISBN: 978-1-879505-89-6 (alk. paper)
1. Acting—Vocational guidance. 2. Acting—Auditions.
I. Title
PN2055.B57 2006
792.02'8023—dc22
2006027730

Cover design and photography by Wade Lageose for Lageose Design
Cover office photograph courtesy of Levene, Neale, Bender,
Rankin & Brill, LLP, Los Angeles

Photograph of Stephen Book by Kevin Langdon Ackerman

Printed and bound in the United States of America

Silman-James Press
1181 Angelo Drive
Beverly Hills, CA 90210

To the memory of my parents, Perle and Lenny Book.

Contents

Introduction

What is your batting average? When you meet with casting directors and agents in order to get auditions or representation, how many times do you get what you want? Your batting average is computed by dividing the number of follow-up calls you get by the number of times you go out. If no one has ever called you back, you're batting zero. If every meeting has led to a follow-up call, you're batting a thousand. What is your batting average?

Many actors "who haven't made it yet" feel that their batting averages are unsatisfactory. They think they know how to conduct themselves in interviews and are confident, yet their batting averages are low. It has never dawned on them that there may be another approach to interviewing. Other actors are afraid of interviews but know it shouldn't be as scary as it is to them to be interviewed. Their batting averages are also unsatisfactory.

How to conduct yourself in an interview is the subject of this book. Learning how you may inadvertently be sabotaging your interviews while doing the exercises presented here should help to eliminate your self-defeating behavior and give you techniques to increase your batting average dramatically. The exercises are sequential, and if you do them in the order in which they are presented, your interviews should get progressively better.

In addition to always seeking employment, actors are always looking to move up—to their first paying jobs, their first agents, their first union jobs, their first guest-star jobs on prime-time TV series, their first Broadway roles, and so forth. Actors on the way up frequently and unconsciously turn off the people whose assistance they need. Doing the exercises in this book and tracking the growth of four actors whose interview transcripts are presented at each step of the process should help you to conduct yourself more effectively in interviews.

The genesis of this book was an interview project I created for actors at a Hollywood workshop in 1992. Some of the exercises are acting exercises and improvisations from Improvisation Technique.[1] Each exercise or improvisation, which requires that you work with no distractions, will specify what your acting focus should be. Other exercises, along with additional material in this book, were specifically created for the interview project and have been refined over the past fourteen years. Each chapter represents the exercises and material covered in one four-hour class. At my workshop the entire interview project takes seven classes.

1

How Do You Present Yourself?

nterview appointments are usually the result of your being submitted to an agent, casting director, or anyone in a position to further your career, such as a director or producer. The submission usually consists of a cover note with your picture and résumé—sometimes a demonstration video of your work is also included. If you submit yourself, it is called a "cold," or unsolicited, submission. Interview appointments can be set up through personal contacts, e.g., recommendations from a producer or director or your uncle Bob who went to college with the agent. When a casting director or agent receives a submission, he or she places it in one of three categories: consider, reject, or call-in—call-ins are the submissions from which he will ask to have face-to-face-meetings or interviews. How to participate in these interviews is the subject of this book.

Workshop Actors' Interviews

The following general interviews are transcripts of interviews simulated in my workshop to begin the interview project. We will track four actors progressing through *The Actor Takes a Meeting* by reading their latest interviews in each chapter. We start with their first interviews, which established a reference for how the actors usually did interviews before they began the project.

The names of the students, other actors, and particular credits have been changed. I played the casting director for a new small independent-film company. Prior to the interviews the actors were told that the company intends to produce seven feature films over the next two years. These interviews are general interviews, intended for the casting director to meet actors new to him and to create a file for future use. I sat behind a table with a chair opposite me for the actors to use. Their pictures and résumés were on the table in front of me. There was a carton on the floor next to my chair.

First Interview — Josh

(*Josh enters. He is 25, 5'11", 165 lbs.*)

Casting Director: Hello, Josh. Have a seat. How are you doing today?

Josh: Fine. You know, another day in L.A.

Casting Director: Another day in L.A.?

Josh: Yes. Not good? Well, let's just say it was a busy day. Monday. (*Pause*)

Casting Director: So, what is your story, Josh?

Josh: Fairly new in town from Texas. Been here two years and a day or so. Though, it seems like forever. Last few years, I have been experiencing a nice, fat, rude awakening as far as my level of where I thought I was and where I actually am. So, it has been a learning experience.

Casting Director: So, these years have been tough?

Josh: Yes.

Casting Director: I'm sorry.

Josh: I guess what doesn't kill you makes you stronger. Someone said that.

Casting Director: That is true. What has been so tough?

Josh: I really have had trouble finding a good agent. There is not a lot of response, generally. Not a lot of *no*'s, just nothing at all.

Casting Director: That would be hard. What do you attribute this to?

Josh: Really, a lot of it is not knowing myself and not having the best habits for getting out and networking and stuff like that. Any success I have had in the past was really bum luck, just being in the right place at the right time. I kind of fooled myself into believing I made it happen, but it was just luck. As far as my acting goes, I have always been consistent. But, networking skills . . . I could be more disciplined and have a stronger work ethic as far as getting out there. I feel like I just have to bang my head against the wall until it cracks.

Casting Director: Is that how it happens?

Josh: Yes. Pretty much. If there isn't a door, I will make one. (*Pause*)

Casting Director: (*Looking at résumé*) Okay. Let's see. You got into *We Were Soldiers*. What did you do in that?

Josh: I played Hank. I was one of the soldiers in Vietnam. It started as a really large, wonderful part, but by the time the whole budget thing went to hell, it ended up being . . . if you look at the film, I was a very-well-paid extra. I spent about three weeks in South Carolina, and it was really great to work with Mel Gibson and Randall Wallace.

Casting Director: Is that where they shot the Vietnam scenes?

Josh: Yes, South Carolina. They flew me out there. To go from nothing to, "We are going to fly you out to South Carolina to meet with the producer. Can you be at the airport in a half an hour?" It was sort of weird. Seven weeks of auditioning. A lot of it was—I kind of stumbled in when I was doing a play at the time. So I went in to read for something, and they said, "No. We are going to read you for a soldier." I meet this wonderful casting director out of New Orleans who works for Paramount, Alicia Russell. We just really hit it off. She really helped out. It was really a great experience, but it was sort of early. It didn't help me to get a real clear image of what the business was about and how really difficult it could be. From then on, I have had to learn that that was kind of a lightning strike and that you have to put in your time. (*Pause*)

Casting Director: (*Looking at résumé*) So, you have been doing theater?

Josh: Yes. Since I have been here, not so much. I have had a lot of schedule conflicts. I have tried, but lately, I haven't gotten much response. It is not like I am going to auditions and people are saying, "Thank you." No one is calling me. So, I have been playing with my image, and I finally came to the conclusion that I have to just be me. That's all. I just redid my résumé and got all new pictures. It's nice.

Casting Director: It's a good photo.

Josh: I guess the best analogy, I was telling this to my sister last night, my picture makes me look like a Ross and I am actually a Chandler. I'm sorry, that is a *Friends* analogy.

Casting Director: Ross is David Schwimmer and you are a Chandler.

Josh: Ross is a rather nice guy, and I have more of an edge and am more of a smart-ass.

Casting Director: Okay. Anything you want to ask me?

Josh: Yes. I'd like to know more about the projects. I heard you are doing several features over the next few years.

Casting Director: Yes.

Josh: It is all the same production company that you are using then? Are you using different directors?

Casting Director: Yes.

Josh: Any of the director deals set yet?

Casting Director: Yes, some are.

Josh: Do you know who any of the directors are?

Casting Director: I can't name them yet. Why?

Josh: Just curious. I make a lot of my decisions about acting in parts if I have the opportunity to work with someone interesting. So, I was just curious. Is it possible for you to tell me about any of the projects?

Casting Director: The first three films are a romantic comedy, a cowboy picture, and a bank-heist. (*Pause*) Anything else?

Josh: Not really. I would like to come in and read for you.

Casting Director: At this point, I am just meeting people and building a file. Casting is about a month away.

Josh: I hope you are going to remember me.

Casting Director: Anything else I can do for you?

Josh: No. Thanks for calling me in.

Casting Director: It was nice to meet you.

Josh: If I do a play, I'll send you an invitation.

Casting Director: Okay.

Josh: Thank you very much.

Casting Director: Thank you. Bye-bye.

(*Josh exits. The casting director drops his picture and résumé in a carton.*)

First Interview — Anthony

(*Anthony enters. He is 44, 5'10," 190 lbs.*)

Anthony: Hi, Stephen, nice to meet you.

Casting Director: Nice to meet you. (*Pause. Looks at résumé*) So, Anthony, let's see, so you have been working a lot?

Anthony: That's right. Theater and film. I am in a play right now. It is called *Lovers and Other Strangers*.

Casting Director: The Joe Bologna play?

Anthony: Yes. Actually, this will be the first time in thirty years that this play has been done in Los Angeles. They usually won't let it be done here, but my manager has secured the rights for it.

Casting Director: It is the first time it has been done out here since when?

Anthony: At least thirty years. It premiered in New York in 1968, and for quite some time they have not allowed it to be run in L.A.

Casting Director: Well, good. Do you have a good part?

Anthony: The lead. Do you know the play?

Casting Director: I have seen showcase scenes from it.

Anthony: I have a great scene that takes place in the bathroom. I am the ultimate denial guy.

Casting Director: Okay.

Anthony: You don't like the theater? I think it is going to be lots of fun. I am very excited about it.

Casting Director: When does it open?

Anthony: The opening-night date isn't set yet. I will send you a flyer.

Casting Director: Okay. *(Pause)* So what have you done in film?

Anthony: I co-starred in *Deep Impact.*

Casting Director: I just saw that on television. What part did you play?

Anthony: They brought me in for a couple of days as one of the astronauts who couldn't cut the mustard. I will be in *State of Siege*, coming out this Christmas. I am the civilian guy who gets carjacked. I say, "This is the third time this month that it happened in L.A."

Casting Director: Okay. Have you done any parts in films where you have had more than one scene?

Anthony: All those parts have lines.

Casting Director: Oh, yes, I am sorry. I got the impression that they—

Anthony: Right now I am up for a lead in the new Spielberg film, and I am playing leads in several student film projects.

Casting Director: The new Spielberg film, good for you. How far along in the process are you?

Anthony: I'm supposed to have an audition next week.

Casting Director: *(Looking at résumé)* What is *Green Lantern?*

Anthony: That was thirty-six episodes of an animated series with James Caan. The Green Lantern is a ten-year-old master spy. I was playing his dad. *(Sarcastic)* I was in a lot of scenes. *(Pause)*

Casting Director: *(Looking at résumé)* I can see you have studied. How old are you?

Anthony: Over forty.

Casting director: How long have you been out here?

Anthony: Actually, on and off, it has been about six years now. I took a long break from the business. I was a "rep rat" on the East Coast when I was younger.

Casting Director: A "rep rat?"

Anthony: I did a lot of repertory theater with Vermont Shakespeare—*Macbeth*, *Iago*. The Bloomsbury Theatre Ensemble in Pennsylvania. I kind of stepped out of the business for seven years, went to Japan and became a PR editor, and got the crazy notion to come back here a while back. (*Pause*) So, this is a new company and you are slated for seven films already? Are there principals involved? Are you the casting guy?

Casting Director: Yes. I'm casting.

Anthony: Is this your first time casting? Were you a staff person or are you used to this?

Casting Director: I've worked at the studios.

Anthony: So, it's another gig?

Casting Director: Yes.

Anthony: Cool. Well, I hope it works out.

Casting Director: Thank you very much. Thanks for coming in.

(*Anthony exits the office. The casting director drops his picture and résumé in the carton.*)

First Interview — Shannon

(*Shannon enters. She is 33, 5'8", 125 lbs.*)

Shannon: Hello, Mr. Book.

Casting Director: Hi, Shannon. Have a seat.

Shannon: Thank you. (*Laughs*)

Casting Director: Excuse me?

Shannon: Oh, it's nothing.

Casting Director: I was just wondering what you were grinning at.

Shannon: Just happy about life. Just happy to be here. Just happy to meet you. (*Pause*)

Casting Director: So, Shannon, what have you been up to?

Shannon: Just getting ready for the holidays. I booked a voice-over yesterday and I am working three days on a SAG industrial, so things are looking good from that point. No TV or films right now, though. As you can see from my résumé, it is not that extensive. I do not have a lot to choose from, but what I have done I have been very good at. I have videotape. Do you need videotape?

Casting Director: No. If we do, we will let you know. (*Looks at résumé*) Would I have seen any of these films?

Shannon: Oh, I'm sorry. Most of those are student-directed films. So, you wouldn't have seen them. But one of the reasons I did them was to work on the characters, to try and find out about myself. I was trying to determine certain roles that I was appropriate for. I took a course that allowed me the opportunity to get people to look at me from afar and make a determination on how they would see me, without even speaking with me.

Casting Director: When did you start acting?

Shannon: About nine years ago. I moved out here and stayed with my brother for a while. He was taking commercial workshop classes, so I did, too, because I thought I could just do commercials out here. After that, I started taking theatrical classes and liked it. So I started actually acting about nine years ago.

Casting Director: You find it worthwhile?

Shannon: I love it. I have continued, basically, nonstop. I've taken at least one class a week for almost the entire time.

Casting Director: I don't mean classes. I mean do you perform as an actor regularly?

Shannon: I mean worthwhile emotionally. Worthwhile for myself? Financially, I haven't made that much money. Last year, I did qualify for benefits from the Guild. I am going to continue to do it, no matter what, because I like acting, performing, and being onstage. So, yes, it is worthwhile in that regard. If money comes out of it, eventually, then it will. If it doesn't, I will continue doing what I am doing.

Casting Director: What was it exactly that made you want to be an actor?

Shannon: I love the process. I have always loved performing and being onstage. When I was a kid, I did a lot of musical theater in high school, and in community theater, and I just wanted to pursue it full-time and see what that felt like.

Casting Director: Okay. Anything you want to ask me?

Shannon: Yes. I understand you are doing seven movies?

Casting Director: Yes, we are.

Shannon: That is incredible. And you're the casting director? Wow. You must be really good at it to get this job. I'm really impressed. What kind of movies are they? What genre?

Casting Director: Romantic comedy, cowboy picture, and a bank-heist.

Shannon: You sound like you have been asked that question all day.

Casting Director: Somewhat.

Shannon: Cowboy picture. Do you like *City Slickers*? That is one of my favorite movies. Is yours a comedy or what?

Casting Director: No, it is like an older Western. It is an existential Western.

Shannon: An existential Western. Wow. Great. It's so fantastic that you are doing adult material. Well, I ride horses. You said you are doing a bank-heist?

Casting Director: Yes.

Shannon: I don't look it, but I can play a vixen very well.

Casting Director: You can play a vixen?

Shannon: Imagine me in a real tight skirt and a real low-cut top. Don't you think I can do it?

Casting Director: Sure. Anything else I can do for you?

Shannon: Let me ask you a question: Can you tell me what sense you get from me as far as—I see you are taking notes—I am not asking you to read me the notes, but how do you see me? When you look at me, what do you see? The reason I am asking that is because I am trying to put it together with other information I have got.

Casting Director: I see a vixen.

Shannon: (*Laughs*) You're funny. Seriously, what kind of part do you see me playing?

Casting Director: Young professional.

Shannon: Exactly! Like a lawyer, or a businesswoman. You get me. Are there any lawyer roles coming up in your movies?

Casting Director: Possibly.

Shannon: Without asking the questions of what they are and what roles are available, are you pretty familiar with the scripts of all of them?

Casting Director: Two haven't been written yet, but the others I am.

Shannon: Are there any of the five that you feel I would be appropriate for?

Casting Director: Sure.

Shannon: Great. Good.

Casting Director: Anything else I can do for you?

Shannon: Call me in to read sometime.

Casting Director: Okay. Do you have a monologue you could do right now?

Shannon: Right now?

Casting Director: Yes.

Shannon: Not at the moment.

Casting Director: Okay. Well, thank you for coming in.

Shannon: Okay. Bye-bye.

(*Shannon exits. The casting director drops her picture and résumé in the carton.*)

First Interview — Lisa

(*Lisa enters. She is 23, 5'4," 112 lbs.*)

Lisa: Hi.

Casting Director: Hi, Lisa. Nice to meet you. How are you?

Lisa: Nice to meet you.

Casting Director: Have a seat.

Lisa: Thank you.

Casting Director: What is the matter?

Lisa: Do I look worried?

Casting Director: Nervous.

Lisa: Really? I'm not. (*Laughs*) I am. (*Laughs*) I'm sorry.

Casting Director: You're nervous?

Lisa: I think a little bit. Trying to talk myself out of it.

Casting Director: There is nothing to be nervous about.

Lisa: I'm okay. How was your summer vacation?

Casting Director: Ah, fine. It was short and I hardly remember it. (*Pause*)

Lisa: Mine was very stimulating. I went to London and it was packed full of intense moments. Before we left, my boyfriend had to go to the emergency room because he had a kidney stone or something, even though they could not find a stone. Point being, that made us late getting to the airport. We got to the airport gate just as they were taking off. Of course, when we got on the plane, my boyfriend couldn't find his passport, so we got kicked off the plane, and we had three hours to find his passport to catch our flight, which had been rerouted to New York. Amazingly, they found the passport on the original flight. So, we took the flight to New York. They had the passport there in London waiting there for him, and it started off just like that. And it was pretty much consistently *boom*, *boom*, *boom*, tons of kinetic energy and events. It was exciting, but it made the trip seem like it was only three days when it was actually eight. So, I guess I am just coming off of that high because it was very exciting and challenging. I don't know what else to say about it. I could tell you tons of stories about it. It was really exciting.

Casting Director: How old are you?

Lisa: Older than I was and younger than I'll be, or something like that. My agent puts me out for sixteen to twenty-three.

Casting Director: Okay. So, you don't want to tell me how old you are?

Lisa: Well, I will tell you. I'm twenty-three.

Casting Director: Okay. How long have you been acting?

Lisa: Pretty much since I could murmur. It has been something that I have always done. I trained in college for four years, and I graduated a year ago, so I have been professionally acting for a year, but the essence of acting has existed since before words coming out.

Casting Director: Before what?

Lisa: Words.

Casting Director: Really. The essence of acting has existed since before words. That is very . . . I have no idea what that means.

Lisa: I'm sorry. Just the knowledge of how acting is, what I am meant to do just seemed to resonate in me when I was very young, and it has consistently been my goal to act. I have pretty much been very focused on attaining that goal, and I went to college to do it and have done everything that my teachers tell me I should, and after being successful with all that stuff, like getting résumés and head shots and into SAG, auditioning, and getting to learn the business, now I am just trying to pursue it further and see what the next step is.

Casting Director: I didn't know there was a next step.

Lisa: I think it would be working.

Casting Director: Oh, working. That would be a good one.

Lisa: Yes. So, it has been an exciting year and educational, but I definitely feel that I am ready to move on and begin acting and put to use everything I have learned.

Casting Director: Okay. What is keeping you from doing it?

Lisa: I don't know. I think if I knew, I would get past it. I don't know if it is a picture or a résumé glitch, or an agent thing, or maybe I don't have the insight. Maybe it is just the longevity that others have had. If I knew what it was, I would just get past it. I just don't know what it is.

Casting Director: Do you have an agent?

Lisa: Yes.

Casting Director: (*Looking at résumé*) Ajax Talent.

Lisa: Yes.

Casting Director: How often do they send you out?

Lisa: My last audition was four months ago.

Casting Director: Hmmm.

Lisa: Exactly. They are very nice to me, but they don't put me up for anything. How am I supposed to get an acting job if they don't get me any chances?

Casting Director: Well, good luck.

Lisa: Well, thank you. I think I will get past this.

Casting Director: Anything you want to ask me?

Lisa: I guess, just specifically, if I might be able to audition for you, if you are in that ballpark?

Casting Director: Well, right now we are going through pictures to see what is what, and we will go from there.

Lisa: Okay. Well, thank you for seeing me. I appreciate your time. Have a good day.

Casting Director: You, too.

Lisa: Thanks.

(*Lisa exits. The casting director drops her picture and résumé into the carton.*)

Follow-Up Questions

You should now respond to the follow-up questions.

What did you observe about the actors during these interviews?

Most actors involved in an exercise interview, either as a participant or an observer, are shaken by what they see. Some actors babble, revealing that they are very nervous or anxious; some actors exhibit defensive behavior as if the interview is so unpleasant they can hardly wait to leave; many actors spend time apologizing for themselves and what they are doing—they speak negatively about their careers. Some actors try to make it seem as if they are more experienced than they are and exaggerate or lie about their credits. Another form of lying is for the actor to become a "yes man," using flattery and manipulation to woo agents or casting directors. Some actors even take on different personas at interviews. Instead of being themselves they become completely different people. Also, many actors do not treat the casting director as a peer. They act subservient to the casting director, practically begging for the person's approval.

What did you observe about the casting director during these interviews?

In these four interview exercises where one person played the role of casting director for multiple interviews, the casting director began to tire, and his increasing fatigue showed up as grumpiness: The casting director was very kind in the first couple of interviews and a little grumpy in the final two. As the interviews went on, the casting director also became a little more transparent, unable to disguise his increasing boredom. For the real casting director the interview is even more difficult because it occurs during a high-pressure workday at the office. The professional casting director has real obligations, such as having to find the right actors for parts and having to deal with producers, directors, agents, staff, and budgets.

How would a casting director or agent feel when faced with the behaviors exhibited by our four actors?

When an actor babbles, how do you think a casting director feels? As if you are wasting his or her time. When an actor is defensive it makes the casting director feel like the teacher who has to make everyone stay after school. Will the casting director want to see that actor again? Probably not. Displays of low self-esteem such as unnecessary apologizing and seeking the casting director's constant approval make the casting director focus on the actor's insecurity. Will the casting director want to place this actor on a high-pressure movie set? Probably not.

In addition, when faced with the insecure and subservient actor, the casting director experiences a feeling of obligation, of having to take care of the actor. The casting director has to reassure the actor that he or she is okay—more work. Will the casting director like this actor? No. If the casting director recognizes an actor's low self-esteem—and it will be recognized—the casting director may feel that it is a waste of time to deal with someone who doesn't think that his or her own career is worthwhile. Will the casting director want to see this actor again? No.

When the actor lies, bullshits, or attempts manipulation, how do you think the casting director feels? Disgusted and ready to run out and take a shower. Will that actor be called back for an audition? Don't count on it. If an actor lies to me, I certainly don't want to see that actor again.

What happens when the casting director is put on a pedestal by the actor? It is not pleasant because he or she knows the pedestal is in place only because of his or her being a casting director. Have you ever been treated as an object? How do you feel about the person who does that to you? Do you want to see that person again? Interviews with neophyte actors are frequently not fun for the interviewer and some are downright drags. These interviews usually result in the actor's picture and résumé being thrown away. At this point in this exercise in my workshop, I empty the carton of pictures and résumés straight into the trashcan.

Your Goal

What should be your goal when you go to a general interview? Some students will say that their goal is to get the job, and I will point out that that's not realistic. Nobody's getting a job in a general interview. Your goal should be to be remembered and get called back for an audition. What you don't want is for the casting director to say, "Thank you very much," and, as soon as you leave, throw your picture in the trash. Casting directors don't keep every picture and résumé just because it was submitted or just because they met the actor—to keep them all would require hundreds of file cabinets. Your goal is to have your picture and résumé put into some kind of "hot" file. Making that your goal carries a lot less pressure than the one of getting a job. So, I suggest you adjust your sights and be realistic.

The interviews by our four actors reveal that they have little or no concept of what should happen in a meeting and why they are seldom successful at playing on a level with the professionals. They are not alone—most actors who haven't made it yet interview just as these four did. We're going to start fixing that right now.

A New Approach

"The definition of insanity is doing the same thing over and over and expecting different results." This quote, attributed to Benjamin Franklin, obviously means that, if you want different results, you have to try something new. For instance, if you have talked about losing weight your whole life and never changed your eating habits, you will always have the same non-result. If you always approach weight loss with a trendy crash diet, you will drop a few pounds, but then gain them back—plus more—and you're insane if you think otherwise. If you truly want different results, you need to change your approach from the get-go. Then, and only then, will you have a shot at different results. This, of course, translates to *if you want to change your batting average at interviews, you have to approach your interviews differently*. This book is about offering you specific ways of changing your behavior and your approach.

Stay alert to your own specific forms of resistance. You may provide yourself with reasons not to accept what we are about to attempt because you've been so caught up in what you've been doing your whole career. Your choices have been comfortable for you, but that doesn't mean they work. It could be that many of the things you think are important are not. Now you have an opportunity to move forward and increase your batting average if you're willing to change some basic behavior patterns at your interviews.

Create an Experience

What does it take for a casting director to remember you and put you in a permanent file? The actor who comes in for an interview and *creates an experience* with the casting director is the one who will be remembered. The casting director will like you and want to see you again. You must take the responsibility to ensure that both of you have a good time. You might be saying, "Oh well, I always do that. I have a very nice response in interviews." But maybe that's not what is really happening. Casting directors mirror back to you whatever you give them. If you project a persona that is not really you, they will intuit this and be polite, maybe even chat with you a little, but they will get you out of their offices as quickly as possible. *You walk out thinking you did well, but you never get called back.* These casting people have chosen to be pleasant because it goes with the gig. But there are a few casting directors who have less patience and won't even pretend to chat with you.

The most important thing you can do in an interview is to make sure the interviewer has a good time with you. Let's begin by substituting different vocabulary for *make sure to have a good time* because this sounds as if you have to manipulate interviewers in some way. Instead let's say that you must make sure they have an experience with you—just an experience, nothing more.

What is an experience? An experience is the effect people have on one another when they come together as equals with spontaneity and authenticity. An experience requires both self-respect and respect for the other. Byproducts of an experience frequently include humor or laughter and the mutual exploration of thoughts and feelings. An experience between an interviewer and an actor happens in the present tense, or, defined in actor terms, is "in the moment."

In the exercise interviews you saw your fellow actors projecting attitudes of negativity and low self-esteem. You saw behaviors that included lying, not listening to the casting director, manipulating the situation, acting like victims, being defensive, and even displaying anger. Being on the receiving end of these attitudes and behaviors makes the interview a burden for the casting director. An experience is not possible under these conditions.

You might assume that the casting director was to be the host of the meeting, and if she/he didn't make you feel comfortable, or ask the right questions, you felt it didn't go well. Change your frame of reference. *Who should be the host?* You, the actor. If you are the host, you'll have to wake the casting director up. He or she will notice the person who takes responsibility for making sure that both of you have a good time. If the casting director has the total responsibility for getting you, the actor, through an interview, that's labor-intensive on the casting director's part. *If you make the casting director work too hard at the interview level, you won't be called back or seen again.* The person who comes in and allows the casting director to relax and have fun is the person who will be remembered. Bill Robinson, a long-time ICM agent, offers, ". . . in the meeting, you're not going to show somebody how talented you are. All they're going to see is your quality. So when you go into that meeting, you can't just go and react, you've got to be passionate, reasonable, and you've got to convince that person, *without verbally saying it*, that you're going to make it anyhow. They have to feel that this person has something special—not just as an actor, but as a person. That he has drive, commitment, an inner strength. You have to go in there and take responsibility. When you walk into a meeting, always think, 'If this doesn't work it's my fault.' What's not going to work is when you think, 'Gee, I hope it works and this person likes me.' After a meeting, it's easy to walk out and say, 'He was a jerk,' and blame it all on the other person. The fact is you've got to take responsibility for yourself. You can't just hope that somehow something nice is just going to happen to you."[1]

In order to begin the process of learning how to create an experience, you need to know what the obstacles are. What mistakes do you and other actors commonly make to ensure that no experience occurs? The three most common stances that actors take to mess up an interview:

> to act as a **Victim**;

> to act with **Inauthenticity**;

> and to act in **Isolation**.

Victim

Playing the role of victim is the greatest obstacle to having an experience with the casting director. In adopting the victim stance, Jack Lee Rosenberg and Beverly Kitean-Morse write that "a person carries a body experience of being 'done to,' of not being in control of situations."[2] When you assume a victim stance, the casting director gets a sensation that you have to be taken care of. This does not imply that he or she has put words to the sensation, but only feels that you are a person who needs maintaining. Do you think the casting director is going to keep the picture and résumé of somebody who has to be coddled? Acting as a victim cripples you. The casting director conducts him or herself like a professional while you act like a helpless incompetent—not anyone the casting director could recommend to a producer or director. The casting director would be fired, along with you. If you observed in the exercise interviews that I, as the casting director, seemed to be waiting for someone to come in and be good, you were not far from wrong. However, it wasn't an audition, and I wasn't waiting for someone to be good. *I was unconsciously waiting for someone I didn't have to nurse along.* If I were a professional casting director, I wouldn't be being paid to be a nurse. And I would truly dislike anyone who made me take care of him or her while I was trying to do my job. It would make my job harder and sap my energy while having nothing to do with my professional work.

Actors most commonly present themselves as victims when they consider themselves beneath the interviewer. These victims acknowledge the interviewer as more important than they are. Victims lose sight of the fact that the casting director wants to like them. The more actors a casting director is impressed with, the quicker the casting director's quotas, or lists, will be filled—and the quicker everyone will get home. Victims think just the opposite—they believe that the interviewer is out to get them and to discover how truly worthless they are. It's no wonder that victims face interviews with trepidation; they think they are going to an inquisition. The only reaction victims ever get is pity and anger, never a callback. We will do exercises to help rid you of your victim stance.

The victim stance can show up in different ways and with varying degrees of intensity. One example of being a victim is waiting for the interviewer to ask questions. Remember, *the casting director does not want to know anything about you that you could provide by answering questions.* The only thing an interviewer wants from you in a general interview is to be *shown* who you are as a person, not *told* who you think you are. Casting directors and agents want to have an experience with you, one in which you delight, intrigue, fascinate, or compel them. If they have that kind of experience with you, they have found out all they need to know.

Sometimes you go to an interview with prepared answers that you readily provide when you get an anticipated question. But there are *no* good prepared answers! There are, also, no good questions. *When the casting director asks you a question, you're in trouble.* The only reason that casting directors or agents ask questions is that you have made them feel as if they have to be hosts. Questions keep the ball rolling or else you'd be sitting in silence. If questions are asked, that means the interviewer has to take care of you—the victim. Consider a talk show like *Letterman* or *Leno.* The guests on those shows who immediately create an experience with the host are the good guests. They allow the host to riff off them, and they never have to answer a single question. Those are the guests you like to watch. Those are the guests who get invited back. But when an interview becomes a question-and-answer segment, you change the channel.

If it is true that the ideal interview is one in which the interviewer doesn't ask any questions, what does that make the interview? Conversation. I suggest that from here on you start thinking of an interview as a conversation or a meeting. By thinking of it as an interview, you are making yourself a supplicant, not an equal, because it implies that you want something from that person. You go to a job interview because you want a job. But we have already decided that it's unrealistic to expect a job from a general interview. All you want is to be remembered, and that only happens when you have an experience with the interviewer. If you say, "I have a meeting today at ten o'clock with the casting director of such and such," you will be on an equal footing with the interviewer and able to create an experience with him or her. Calling it a conversation or meeting will serve as a better frame of reference for you.

Résumé

Another sure sign that you are in trouble in a meeting is when the interviewer takes time to study your résumé. Casting directors, agents, managers, producers, and directors get a sense of an actor's professional standing from a very quick glance at a résumé, no more than five to fifteen seconds. Aside from those few seconds, if the casting director spends most of your interview studying your résumé, it means you're not making it. There's nothing going on between you that's an experience, and you are not holding his or her interest. The casting director is bored and has nowhere to go but to read your résumé. When casting directors talk to you about what's on your résumé, they are reaching to come up with conversation. They won't thank you for making them work harder. In other words, you've made them take care of you again. *In the effective interview, the casting director doesn't look at your résumé.* A résumé presents information that can be looked at before or after your interview. Information is a great deadener of authentic experience.

Best Behavior

Making sure that you are on your best behavior is another sign of being a victim. It creates in you a stance similar to that of criminals who are convinced they can lie their way out of any interrogation, and this certainly would not contribute to having an experience. Being on your best behavior implies that the interview, from your point of view, is about your manners. Actually it is, but maybe not in the way you think. In contemporary society, manners refer to the way you hold your fork or a man's opening a door for a woman, or the actor respectfully answering all questions. But this is not "manners" in the old sense of the word, manners as a reference for the moral aspects of conduct. Socrates argued that the greatest wisdom, the best manners, allowed one to differentiate between good and evil. Being on your polite and best behavior in an interview is ultimately—and I am stretching to make a point here—evil because it will contribute to the interviewer's having to take care of you and, ultimately, disliking you.

Many beginning actors approach interviews with their best behavior because they think it communicates what nice people they are. This is important to them because they assume that there are many actors who are equally talented, so in order to tip the balance in their favor, they communicate that they are good people—professional, malleable, agreeable, etcetera. In fact, behaving in this manner produces quite the opposite effect. At the interview, it's about authenticity and having an experience. At the audition, it's about preparation, talent, and technique. In the end, it is always about the work. If you are a "nice" person, that will always be communicated along the way. If you have to focus on communicating or demonstrating that you are a nice person, the interviewer will ask you to "get off the bus."

Personal Problems

Talking about your personal and career problems is another sure sign of being a victim. Actors who do this may have noble intentions but will have disastrous results. They think that by talking about their problems they are sincerely communicating how much they want to be successful actors and how hard they will work if given the opportunity. Casting people know how tough it is to get ahead as an actor and don't need you to tell them. They also assume that every actor they meet will work hard (unless the interview reveals otherwise). A professional wouldn't even consider working hard to be an issue, much less talk about it. Instead of respecting you for sharing your problems, the interviewer may consider you a loser. Besides, how can anyone have a positive experience with you if you are bringing all your problems to the party? Dan Shiner, who casts television features, relates, "I've seen a lot of actors talk themselves out of a job. When a director initiates general small talk, they go into great detail about their personal life and problems. This *guarantees* that the person will not get the job. I had a guy come in once and talk for half an hour about the child-custody case he was fighting with his wife. He then gave a great reading. But the director said, 'There's no way I can spend five weeks on the set with that guy.' So if they ask how you are doing, just say, 'Fine.' I don't want to be harsh about it, but people don't want to hear about other people's problems." He adds, "We are here to do a job."[3]

Another version of this problem is when you blame your lack of success on your agent. No one likes people who blame everybody else for their problems. Why are you even talking about your lack of success?

Awkward Laughter

If something isn't funny, don't laugh at it. Frequently, when victims are uncomfortable, they cover it up with laughter, which only makes the interviewer uncomfortable. With some people, a giggle may be charming, but never when it comes as a cover-up for real feelings. Those giggles are not amusing, charming, or enticing. They simply communicate how uncomfortable you are, and that makes the interviewer uncomfortable as well.

Low Energy

When you do an interview and your energy is low, you are presenting yourself as a victim. It is impossible to have an authentic experience when you are approaching it with low energy. Low energy is a form of hiding. Victims love to hide. They think that if they can't be seen, they can't be hurt.

Inauthenticity

Lying

Did you ever notice that when someone lies to you, you usually know it? You may not consciously know it at the moment it happens, but you get a sensation that something is wrong. Your body feels uncomfortable. Sometimes you know immediately that you are being lied to, and sometimes, because of a persistent and negative feeling, you figure it out later. *Nobody likes somebody who lies to him or her.* If you lie to casting directors, they will get negative feelings and will probably know that you are lying and will not like you because of it. They will not want to see you again, and your picture and résumé will end up in the trash. You won't even know that your interview was a bust because interviewers will not confront you over the lie.

There are different forms of lying, and all of them create negative effects. The most common form is "lying up." This occurs when an actor makes a credit seem to be more than it is. Promoting yourself through lying is inauthentic. If you were an extra or an "under five" and you attempt to make it seem that you were a principal on a TV show or in a movie, the interviewer will know that you are lying. If you have gotten a call to audition for a part and you refer to this audition as an offer, that's lying up, too.

"Lying down" is just as inauthentic. "Lying down" is making a credit seem less than it is. The perpetrator is less aware of lying than the actor who lies up. This is because the actor "lying down" thinks it's a display of his humility, which is, of course, a good trait. Wrong! Here is an exaggerated example of lying down.

Actor: So I've been working on a few projects. Nothing too interesting. But, you have to pay the bills, you know?

Interviewer: What were some of these projects?

Actor: I did a little work for Spielberg.

Interviewer: His new feature that just finished shooting?

Actor: Yeah.

Interviewer: That's great. Were you a principal? How many scenes did you have?

Actor: I was in every scene. I was the lead.

At this point, the interviewer is not only unimpressed with the actor's humility, he wants to kill him. "Lying down" is inauthentic because it is a charade and a form of manipulation. No one likes to feel manipulated.

Lying up or down are forms of selling yourself. When you attempt to sell yourself to the interviewer, the interviewer will put up a boundary for protection. You have experienced this whenever an overzealous salesman has tried to sell you anything. You didn't trust the salesman and you put up a boundary to keep him at a distance. When you lie up or down, you erect a giant obstacle to having any kind of authentic experience with the interviewer.

Another negative effect of lying is that it affects your acting. The more honest and authentic an actor is in his personal and business life, the more honest and authentic he is in his character portrayals and his overall approach to acting. Actors who lie are usually false in their performances because their bodies frequently display inauthenticity. In addition to a poor believability factor, inauthenticity is an enemy of presence. John Levey, casting director for *ER*, relates: "[Actors] must learn to bring their *authentic self* to their work. Most actors I know are strategizing and hiding—relying on tricks they've had success with in the past and pretending to be the people they're supposed to be inhabiting. That's not doing your work, that's relying on how great your eyes are, how sharp your smile is, how great you look in an A-line skirt. That's not the answer. Those are all wonderful attributes, but drawing from the well of truth and exploring how to get more and more of your authentic self into your work is doing the work. Hiding behind the various successful masks that you've used in the past isn't doing the work, it's faking people out. Most actors fake people out." He adds, "Find a way to roll with what you actually are instead of trying to hide it. Part of what we do in a casting session is say: 'Can we spend a whole day with this person—or five years with this person?'"[4]

Unnecessary Questions

Some actors will ask questions in the interview for which they don't need answers. Even if the interviewer says, "Do you have any questions?" *never ask a question if you don't need the answer.*

Even if you feel you need to have the answer, you probably don't. Besides, if there is anything vital to know, your agent can call to get an answer. Or, you can wait until the interviewer shows further interest in you. If it is not imperative that you ask a question, asking the question is inauthentic. Actors will ask questions because they want to seem interested or they want to extend the interview. When you want to show the interviewer that you are interested, you are performing based on what you think will impress the interviewer. To try deliberately to make an impression is to perform and is inauthentic. It is a lie and self-destructive. Interviewers are not impressed. They are annoyed that you are manipulating them and wasting their time asking irrelevant questions.

There are appropriate questions to ask an agent *after* he or she has offered to represent you. Some of these questions may be: What kind of roles do you see me going out for? How many clients do you represent? May I call in daily or weekly? Will you be representing me for stage work as well as TV and film? How about commercials? Do you "hip pocket" clients (represent without signing)? However, asking any of these questions before agents indicate they would like to represent you may kill any interest in you because you have appeared naive, foolish, and presumptuous.

Compliments

Complimenting an interviewer will probably turn the interviewer off immediately. It's inauthentic and you may only be doing it to get in the interviewer's good graces. It can be a form of manipulation, which will be resented. There are actors who start an interview with a director or producer by complimenting his or her films, even if they have not seen these films. In some cases these actors do not even know which films the director or producer has made. In every one of these situations the director or producer knows the actor is lying or trying to manipulate them. The actor makes the director or producer feel like an object, and the interview is off to a horrendous start. If you really admire a director or producer's work, then mention that, *if you have something specific to say*. "I was really challenged by the theme of your last film. It made me think about . . ." Generic gushing will be taken as a form of manipulation. If you are called back to discuss your possible involvement with a project or script, avoid flattery and say something truthful about the project, something specific that you took away from the script.

Response to Victim

When the actor presents him or herself as a victim the interviewer is forced to become inauthentic also. If the actor is a victim, interviewers have to become caretakers and can't be themselves. The actor's neediness puts an undue burden on any interviewer, who will have to work harder and put on a performance in order to marshal the two of you through the interview. The interviewer doesn't like having to be in performance mode: Putting on a performance is tiring and feels dirty. Judith Holstra, who was the casting director for *48 Hrs.* and the first season of *Thirtysomething*, explains that an actor's neediness upsets her "because I feel that I should be doing something for them other than what I am doing."[5] Why would she want to work with someone who makes her feel guilty? Frequently, neediness, and victim stances are forms of manipulation. When the interviewer is manipulated into taking care of you, he or she knows it and doesn't like it. Manipulation is inauthentic.

Isolation

Telling Stories

Many actors prepare riffs to use in an interview. This is both inauthentic and reflects actors as victims. They don't understand that an interview is about having an experience with the interviewer.

They think it is about telling how interesting they are (inauthentic). They have prepared the riffs to make sure they have something interesting to say (victim).

Most prepared riffs are stories about the actor on a particular job or those from his personal life. When an actor talks about something from the past, be it an acting job or a teacher who inspired him in high school or college, no one is going to have an experience because the interviewer wasn't present at the past activity. The actor is making the interviewer an audience. Audiences are traditionally anonymous and replaceable. When you turn someone into an audience, that person is no longer involved with you as an individual. It is impossible for the two of you to have an experience together in the present tense under those conditions. In addition, while you are telling your story, the interviewer is free to think thoughts that may have nothing to do with your story, splitting off to think about what to have for lunch or sitting back and judging you. On the other hand, when the actor and interviewer are in an experience together, the interviewer is not isolated.

Reaction

Another form of isolation occurs when the actor reacts to an interviewer's mood.

Interviewers are human and have good and bad days. You don't know what's going on in their lives, and they may bring their stress to your meeting. If you react to their negativity, you will only reinforce it. A common reaction to their negativity is to blame them for the unpleasant interview, even if it isn't spoken out loud. The actor who creates an experience with the interviewer will help the interviewer forget personal problems. That actor will be remembered and called back. It's simply bad luck when you encounter a negative interviewer. You can either react to it and waste your meeting or see it as an opportunity to have a very successful meeting. The choice is yours.

Intimidation

Occasionally, an interviewer's negativity will take the form of intimidation. You will feel bullied. How can you handle that? By staying centered, present, and authentic, you will not feel compelled to react. If you remain a victim during the period of intimidation, it will only support and encourage further intimidation. Also, if you try to manipulate the interviewer, the intimidation will be heightened. Your focus when facing an intimidating interviewer is to remain grounded. It will turn the meeting around, and the interviewer will appreciate and remember you.

This chapter and the first exercise interviews are designed to get your attention and to get you to examine your own behavior at interviews. You may be puzzled and frustrated because all the things I suggest you do not do may be exactly what you have been doing. But don't worry—it is fairly easy to change your interview behavior with just a few exercises. In the next chapter, we shall begin transforming your behavior—working to help you lose your victim stance, be authentic, and create an experience with the interviewer.

But before moving on to the next chapter you may want to do the general interview exercise that the four actors did earlier in the chapter. It is not necessary for you to do this exercise in order to move forward, but you may find it helpful to understand how you currently conduct yourself at interviews. It is better to do this exercise with a friend and simulate an actual interview, but if this is not possible, you will still benefit by having read the examples.

General Interview Exercise #1

One of you will play the role of the interviewer and the other the actor. Then you will reverse roles and do another interview. The interviewer should sit behind a table or desk with a chair for the actor on the other side of the desk. To get the most out of the exercise, you should behave as closely as possible to the way you do in an actual interview. This will require honesty on your part. Just do your average interview: not your worst, nor your best.

Your friend will first play the role of casting director for a new small independent-film company. The company intends to produce seven feature films over the next two years. These interviews are general interviews, intended for the casting director to meet actors new to him and to create a file for future use. The casting director has the actor's picture and résumé on the desk. The casting director conducts the interview according to personal experiences of being interviewed in similar situations. The interview begins when you walk into the casting director's space. When the casting director feels it is about the time a real casting director would thank the actor for coming in and end the interview, he should do so. The interview ends with the actor's exit.

Then apply the lessons that you have learned from this first chapter to a discussion of each other's interviews.

2

Losing the Victim

When does your victim stance kick in? The moment you hear you have an appointment for an interview or an audition, your defense system—which includes your victim stance and your inauthenticity—starts its self-destructive process. Your feelings of being a victim and any resulting inauthenticity continue right up to the appointment, including that very dangerous period—waiting in the outer office to go into the interview—and, of course, the interview itself. For some, this period may even continue after the interview. We will now work on creating an antidote to your victim stance.

Who's Interviewing Whom?
Part One

The following two paragraphs are best absorbed if you turn them into an improvisation with a friend. The directions are written for you to work alone; therefore, if you improvise with a friend, have your friend actually play the part of Steven Spielberg. Go with the directions as written. Do it a second time, reversing roles. If you cannot do this, then visualize yourself in the situation.

Imagine that you are in the waiting room at Steven Spielberg's offices waiting for an appointment with Spielberg. He is casting leading roles in his next mega-movie, and you and the other actors in the room with you have been recommended to him as being right for these roles. If you are doing this as an improv, your acting focus is to be yourself, behaving and feeling the way you would under these circumstances. If you are imagining this, picture doing what you would do while waiting, and feel what you would feel. Get into the mindset, feelings, and behavior of the way you would naturally respond to this type of situation. What objects would you have with you? Mentally arrange yourself and your objects (purse, Filofax, Palm Pilot, portfolio, etcetera) as if you were really in this situation. Visualize other actors waiting and a receptionist at her desk.

Now after three to five minutes imagine hearing Spielberg speaking to his office staff in the adjoining rooms. In a voice loud enough for the actor(s) to hear, he says, "We're really behind schedule. There are so many of them. Call Ovitz and see what Tom Hanks wants. Reschedule my lunch with Meryl. I want to see the costume plates tomorrow morning."

You get the idea—high-power show-business talk. Then, after another minute, picture Spielberg walking in and out of the waiting room, looking busy. He gets something from the waiting room: a file or a cup of coffee, for instance. While walking, he casually looks the actors over. He says to all of you, "I'm sorry, we're running a little late. I'll be with you in a minute." Spielberg goes back into his office. After another two minutes, picture him returning and announcing that he is ready to see you. The visualization or improv ends.

Follow-Up Questions

Would you say that the behavior you visualized or improvised was authentic for you in that situation?

Is that how you would probably feel and behave while you were waiting?

Did you have the feelings that would normally accompany you in that situation?

How did you feel? How did those feelings manifest or reveal themselves?

Did you have additional emotional responses and accompanying feelings?

Most actors who have not yet made it, and even some who have, will experience or feel nervous, anxious, scared, suspicious, tense, impatient, annoyed, and even nauseated. Some will feel isolated because they feel outclassed, as in, "What am I doing here? This is Steven Spielberg and these people are probably real actors. How did I get this meeting? This is never going to work." This feeling is an example of feeling "one-down" from everyone else; it is a pure victim stance. These feelings will frequently affect the actor's behavior. Some actors become quiet and fidgety or jittery, sit rigidly with perfect posture, pace, become hyper aware of their breathing, talk incessantly, huddle in corners, sigh a lot, become class clowns, or feel unattached to their own bodies. If the feelings you have during this waiting period are, for the most part, negative, you will not feel confident or good about yourself. If you are waiting in a group, your negative feelings will usually be exacerbated. Do you think they are conducive to having a successful interview/meeting? Of course not.

Waiting in a room with others contributes to an actor's stress. Some actors become irritable knowing that they are being watched by the competition. When in this situation, some actors will unconsciously behave in strange ways. One actor might ostentatiously take out sides, spreading them all over the floor, and begin to prepare for an audition; another might initiate excessive or overbearing conversation with another actor or even with everyone in the room. Even if you understand that this kind of behavior is merely "their bullshit," it can still have a negative and intimidating effect on you. Instead of relaxing and focusing, or catching up on your reading, or balancing your checkbook, or comfortably chatting with someone next to you, you get caught up in the drama as you develop an attitude of suspicion and resentment. You would love to tell that obnoxious actor, "You know, you should just sit down and shut up." The more the inappropriate behavior continues, the more tense the other actors in the room become. Some are participating in the drama and others are trying to block it out.

In the middle of all this Spielberg makes an appearance to get some coffee, and he sees you in passing. Even though your interview has not yet begun, he, naturally, starts assessing you the moment he sees or hears you. Sometimes an actor will commence inappropriate behavior to get attention: e.g., start a conversation with Spielberg, complain about the delay, or perform or act out in some fashion. When an actor does this, it usually leads to a director's getting rid of that actor. Even if he meets with the actor, he will probably dislike him or her before the meeting starts. Why? The actor's inappropriate behavior reeks of manipulation. It is the manipulation of a terribly insecure victim who wants to be noticed. When Spielberg spots that inauthentic behavior, and he will because that behavior always calls attention to itself, he will think, "This guy is an amateur. Get rid of him."

Inappropriate behavior to get any director's attention is down-right intrusive to the director and his/her staff and the other waiting actors. The other actors have to respond to the behavior with thoughts such as, "Look at that phony. I am suspicious of him. I have to block him out. I have to ignore him." But why should anyone have to deal with another actor at an important time like this? It is intrusive for the director because the interviews have not yet started and he does not want to have to deal with a manipulative actor in the waiting room.

Who's Interviewing Whom?
Part Two

Now do another improv with a partner or imagine yourself in a similar situation, except this time make the interviewer the director Martin Scorsese. But this time, make an attitude adjustment. While you are waiting for your meeting, assume the attitude that *you are there to interview Scorsese to decide whether or not you will allow him to cast you.* The meeting will then be for you to see if *you* want to give *him* the opportunity to cast you. All of the external aspects of the waiting-room situation, including Scorsese's moving in and out, are the same as in the Spielberg situation.

Follow-Up Questions

After the exercise, ask yourself, "How did I feel this time?"

How did those feelings manifest or reveal themselves?

Did you have additional emotional responses and accompanying feelings?

This time, though, all the waiting actors feel much more aware, comfortable, relaxed, calm, curious, and confident. All the negative feelings and any inauthentic behavior from the previous exercise have disappeared. From Scorsese's point of view, everyone appeared professional. At the Spielberg interview, everyone appeared nervous, uncomfortable, and inauthentic, like orphans about to be checked out by prospective parents. Spielberg wasn't looking forward to meeting any of you. This time, though, everyone looked relaxed, interesting, and energized, and Scorsese felt there was potential and he looked forward to meeting with all of you.

Summary to Who's Interviewing Whom?

Your *choosing to interview directors, casting directors, producers, and agents* is a simple tool that helps you get rid of your showing that you want the part, audition, or representation. Acting as if you want something increases your victim stance. Of course you want the part, but *you mustn't act as if you want the part*! Don't want anything. Changing your attitude rewires your victim stance. A victim stance with its accompanying negative feelings comes from a sense of being one-down from the interviewer. You see him as more important than you. When you meet with someone as a victim, it brings out the worst in you. When you want something from someone, you have a hidden agenda and perform too easily. Performing is inauthentic as it covers up the truth. Performing is insidious and is seen and heard by the interviewer as lying. When you have a hidden agenda you become inauthentic, which turns off all interviewers. But if you put the focus on "interviewing them," you have become their equal. If you did both parts of this exercise as improvs, you just had an experiential taste of the difference between feeling one-down and equal. The more you can learn not to want anything from interviewers, the more comfortable you will be with them. It's obvious that you are an actor and would like the interviewer to call you back. That's a given. Everyone in the room knows that. So get off it—let it go.

A good example of wanting versus not wanting the job is found in the movie *Tootsie*. At the beginning, Dustin Hoffman as Michael is desperate for work. At one audition, he even says to a director, "I can be taller. I can be shorter." His victim stance alternates between neediness and defensiveness. But when he becomes Tootsie and feels secure, all his neediness disappears and he moves on to achieve all the success he ever wanted.

If you are thinking it's inauthentic to say, "I don't want the job," when you obviously do want the job, you are wrong. Of course you want the job, but you should stop focusing or obsessing on wanting the job. You must adopt the *attitude* that you don't want anything. You are taking this meeting because it's propitious for your career, because it's fun and exciting to meet new people, and because it's good to network. It's especially silly to want a job at this point because no one is in a position to hire you at a first interview. Even Steven Spielberg or Martin Scorsese is not going to cast you from a first meeting. The minute you decide not to want anything you will feel a sense of freedom. Tom Parziale, a top manager and president of Visionary Entertainment, tells his clients to go into meetings as if they were leaving them, as if there was nothing more the clients can do to influence getting what they want.

Interviewing your interviewers is a tool you should employ from the moment you hear you have a meeting. Keep renewing this attitude as your meeting draws closer. If you are meeting with a casting director, your attitude should be that you are there to see if you want to give him or her the opportunity to call you in for an audition. If you are meeting with an agent, your attitude should be that you are there to see if you want to give him or her the opportunity of representing you.

When you adopt this attitude you also have to adopt the feeling that you want to like them and give them the opportunity to represent or hire you. Be aware that you don't change "interviewing them" into a power trip for yourself.

Shannon: I am not nervous at all interviews but, I know if I were meeting Spielberg, I would be shaking and sweating like I did in the exercise. Will this calm down my nervousness as much as possible?

Book: Did that disappear in part two?

Shannon: Yes.

Book: You should also consider that frequently you are not aware that you are going into your victim stance or becoming manipulative. If you start to feel awkward, nervous, or pushy, you are probably entering the inauthenticity zone. Step back and remind yourself that you do not want anything.

Josh: So, the time out in the waiting room is almost as important as the meeting?

Book: The time that is important begins the moment you hear that you have the meeting. That is sometimes a week earlier. That is when you begin your victim stance and your inauthenticity. As the meeting gets closer the stakes get higher, building to when the meeting is five minutes away. Victims don't become victims the moment they walk in the door. Victims live the lives of victims. Addressing that issue is much larger than addressing its manifestations in your career, which is what we are doing here. As a result of doing these exercises you will be much more aware of the entire process from the moment you get that phone call. And you will definitely change the way you conduct yourself at the meeting.

Tell a Truth

Who Starts the Meeting?

You are finally called in to the interviewer's office. We will now explore a focus to be used the very moment the meeting starts.

Focus: Tell a Truth

To *tell a truth* means that as soon as you finish saying hello to the interviewer, you must state an absolute truth about something in the office. It cannot be an opinion or a compliment. *It must be a fact.* It can be totally mundane, e.g., "The walls of your office are blue; Your desk is brown; That's a fountain pen; There's a stack of pictures on your desk."

The interviewer starts most meetings with actors who haven't made it yet with a consistent and familiar feeling. If you arrive at the meeting, say hello, and then tell a truth, there will be a significant and pleasant shift in the interviewer's mood. The interviewer will relax because he or she is no longer responsible for being a host. Also, when you start the meeting with a statement that is absolutely true, the interviewer will experience a sense of authenticity about you and relax further.

You are probably coming up with reasons why this focus won't work. Try to stay open, especially now that you have nothing at stake.

General Interview Exercise #2

We are now going to do a second interview exercise similar to the first. Again, it is not necessary for you to do this exercise in order to absorb the lessons. You can just read through the exercise and then read the transcripts of the actors who participated in my workshop. Again, you will make faster progress by participating in the exercise with a partner. If you have a partner, go through the exercise twice—first as the actor and then as the interviewer.

Setup

This time the person conducting the interview will play the part of an agent, whom you have come to see because you are seeking representation. You have a few new tools to employ for this interview:

- While waiting for your name to be called, remember that you are waiting to meet the agent to see if you want to give him the opportunity of representing you.

- During the meeting adopt the attitude that you don't want anything from the agent. It follows that if you don't want anything, you won't have to sell anything.

- When your meeting starts, after you both have said hello, tell a truth.

To the interviewer: Respond to the actor's statement of truth at the beginning of the interview. The actor should respond to your response and a conversation will begin. When you feel that the initial conversation has ended, and you feel that you have become the host of the meeting, drop your head to look at the résumé. As soon as this happens, end the interview. Also, if you feel that you are being lied to or manipulated, no matter how subtly, end the interview. I end the interview by making a buzzing sound.

Here are fourteen very short interviews from our workshop interview project—the final four interviews are those from the actors who are being tracked throughout this book.

Workshop Actors' Interviews

General Interview Exercise #2 — Mark

Book: Mark?

Mark: Yes.

Book: Come on in.

Mark: Hi.

Book: How are you?

Mark: That is a swivel chair.

Book: It is. I love it.

Mark: You can work in like three different positions and zip around the room.

Book: I know. There is only one problem.

Mark: What is that?

Book: There is nothing over there for me to do.

Mark: You could move the desk.

Book: I tell you, this floor sometimes is slick and slippery.

Mark: Well, that will get you over to that Picasso painting faster.

Book: *Buzz!*

Comments

Book: Do you know why he was buzzed out? The lie. There is no Picasso over there. He made it up in order to have a truth line. You don't want your truth line to be a lie of any kind. Up to there he was okay. What was your first line of truth?

Mark: The chair.

Book: The swivel chair. How mundane can you get? Yet, I was totally comfortable and enjoyed the chat. I had a sense this might go somewhere.

General Interview Exercise #2 — Laura

Book: Hi, Laura.

Laura: Hi. You have blue paint.

Book: I beg your pardon?

Laura: You have blue paint. Have you been painting?

Book: No. *Buzz!*

<u>Comments</u>

   Book: She could have been more specific with her statement of truth. She said, "You have blue paint." That confused me. An accurate statement of truth would have been, "There is blue paint on your desktop." That is true and would have been an invitation for me to respond. Then she went to a question, "Have you been painting?" In this exercise, don't ask questions until you see what happens. Say your sentence of truth and wait to see what happens. When your body senses that the agent is not going to say anything, keep going. Either expand on that truth or state another truth. Don't ask questions. Interviewers do not like being asked questions. It means they have to work.

   Laura: When I said, "You have blue paint," I gestured at the paint spot on your desk. I thought that was kind of replacing "on your desk," because I was pointing at it. Is that not okay?

   Book: You are counting on me to be looking where you are, and when I am an interviewer, and especially at the beginning of the meeting, I am finishing up the previous person's notes or glancing at your résumé, and I am not fully attentive yet. That frequently happens. You can't count on interviewers giving you their complete attention at the very start of your meeting. In this case, I didn't see the gesture, only heard the line, and the trouble began.

General Interview Exercise #2 — Linda

Linda: Hi, Stephen.

Book: Hello, Linda. Nice to meet you. Have a seat.

Linda: Nice to meet you. What a rustic table you have here.

Book: Yes, it is rather rustic. It is called cheap. We are in the midst of moving and this is all temporary furniture.

Linda: You have some decorations.

Book: Yes. It is kind of au natural.

Linda: I see you are drinking coffee.

Book: I am drinking water. I wish I had some coffee. Do you have any coffee with you?

Linda: Actually, I don't.

Book: *Buzz!*

Comments

Book: Why did I buzz her? Her response to "Do you have any coffee with you?" was "Actually, I don't." She used the word "actually," and it scared me. Linda, do you have any coffee with you? Yes or no? Why would you say *actually*? Everybody must realize that I work this out in the moment I'm explaining it to you. I do not sit here analyzing everything you say. I just have a body feeling. I refer to that body feeling as an "alert." It alerted me. Then, for your edification, I take the time to figure out what went wrong for you.

General Interview Exercise #2 — Andrew

Book: Hello.

Andrew: Hello. You're eating potato chips.

Book: I am eating potato chips. Excuse me. I haven't had any lunch today.

Andrew: I love potato chips.

Book: Do you want one?

Andrew: No thank you. I just had a big lunch. (*Pause*)

Book: So.

Andrew: So. (*Pause*) How are you doing?

Book: Pretty good. *Buzz!*

Comments

Book: When he said "the potato chips," there was this beat of honest, pleasant conversation around the potato chips. Then it dropped dead and there was a pause and he then went to, "How are you doing?" Instead of that question he would have been better off to tell another truth. The moment your body tells you that you are in trouble, that is when you say the second truth. With practice, you anticipate that moment so you are in front of that moment.

General Interview Exercise #2 — Dorian

Dorian: Hi. I'm Dorian.

Book: Hi. Nice to meet you.

Dorian: The chair is cold.

Book: The chair is cold?

Dorian: I'm sorry. Yes. A little bit.

Book: *Buzz!*

Comments

Book: She had a shot. "The chair is cold." That was fine. I went with it, despite the fact that it was a complaint and not a truth we shared, but her isolated truth. Then she immediately went into an apology, "I'm sorry." My body feeling at that moment was that she was saying, "Oh great exalted one. I am so sorry to insult you by saying you have provided me with a cold chair." That is the essence of the communication I received. Victim. I am going to have to take care of you. Avoid apologies.

General Interview Exercise #2 — Christina

Christina: Stephen Book?

Book: Hello.

Christina: Nice to meet you.

Book: Nice to meet you.

Christina: It is chilly out.

Book: Is it?

Christina: Do they keep it nice and warm in here in, your office?

Book: Yes. Pretty warm in here.

Christina: I am heading up to Canada on the nineteenth, and I bet it is pretty wet and windy up there, too. (*The spaghetti strap of her top slips down her shoulder and Christina adjusts it back in place.*) Oh. Sorry.

Book: *Buzz!*

Comments

Book: The first line of truth was about something that I technically had no knowledge of, "It is chilly out." That is a line of truth about something outside of my experience, something outside of my room. I am inside. What do I know about what is going on outside? Keep the truth inside the room so we can share it. Then when your strap slipped . . .

Christina: I know, and I go, "Sorry."

Book: Instead of just fixing it, you fixed it and apologized. What's to apologize for?

Christina: I have no idea.

Book: This reveals that deep inside you is a victim, which will reveal itself in little things you won't be aware of.

General Interview Exercise #2 — Brian

Book: Hello, Brian

Brian: Hey, Stephen.

Book: Hi.

Brian: Nice to meet you.

Book: Nice to meet you.

Brian: You are taping this?

Book: Yes, I am.

Brian: I will try to be on my best behavior.

Book: *Buzz!*

Comments

Book: We are already in trouble. First of all, before you even sat down, I disliked you. You said, "Hey, Stephen!" That "hey" gave me a sense of inauthenticity about you. If I have to break down why I had that body feeling, I would say that you were assuming a familiarity that doesn't exist between us. If you go into a first meeting at a bank to get a mortgage and say, "Hey, Mr. Smith," you would create a negative effect. It is assuming a familiarity that is not real. That is a manipulation. I let that go because, in the exercise, I wanted you to get the first line of truth out. Then what happened? You asked about the tape recorder and then said, "I will be on my best behavior." Why? Are you a bad little boy? Are you a little victim that can't be himself? Get it?

Brian: It was humor. It was quality humor.

Book: Now you may be in denial. Most people are in denial about their victim stance. It is pretty frightening at first.

General Interview Exercise #2 — Tracy

Tracy: Hi.

Book: How do you do? Have a seat.

Tracy: I am cold.

Book: You are? It will warm up in here.

Tracy: I will just keep my coat on. You have a beard.

Book: I do. I do. It keeps me warm.

Tracy: This is the perfect time of year for it.

Book: Except the ice gets caught in it, but there is no ice in California.

Tracy: True. Food can be a problem, too, I bet—like spaghetti.

Book: I usually use silverware when I eat.

Tracy: Me, too.

Book: Good. (*Pause*) So, Tracy . . . *Buzz!*

Comments

Book: You needed to say the second truth. The beat ended. My head was going down to the picture and résumé. I was reaching for it. I was doing it very slowly, trying to give you a chance, but you didn't jump in. In addition, something was wrong right at the beginning.

Tracy: The "I'm cold?"

Book: Right. It is a complaint.

Tracy: Right. It was my truth but not our truth.

Book: Right. Make your first line of truth about something that is true for both of us. Keep it in the office.

General Interview Exercise #2—Wayne

Wayne: Hi, Mr. Book.

Book: Hi. Have a seat.

Wayne: You have high ceilings in this room.

Book: Very high. Very high.

Wayne: You have a little square cutout on your desk here.

Book: I know. Someone has been doodling there.

Wayne: Very colorful mug.

Book: Yes it is. It is a rainbow mug.

Wayne: They're bright things.

Book: *Buzz!*

<u>Comments</u>

Book: Wayne, since you have come into the room, you have looked very happy. What are you happy about?

Wayne: It is the way I feel.

Book: I don't believe you.

Wayne: I'm not a miserable person.

Book: I just don't believe you. I am going to ask you again. Is that the truth? You feel that happy when you come into this room? I was looking at you in the audience before the interview, and you didn't look that happy.

Wayne: I really did. I did. You know you are asking something that, as I thought about it, I felt happy. Maybe it was sales training where you learn to come in being happy and smiling.

Book: Bingo. That is the truth. When I said, "Since you came in here, Wayne, you have been so happy. What are you happy about?" You said, "Because I feel happy." You were telling me a lie. The truth is what you just told me. "I have been trained in being a salesman to do what you just said, 'to come in being happy and smiling.'" That is the truth.

Wayne: I really hadn't thought about it. I mean—

Book: I know. None of you lies from ill will. None of you lies because you are devious. You have been trained to lie by yourselves and your parents and the business. Awhile ago there was a hullabaloo about the writer of the TV series *Felicity*. She got busted for lying about her age and trying to pass herself off as a college-age student. That is not about her. That is about the business. The [show] business trained her to lie. But notice how unconditional the lying is. When I ask you, as your coach, a straight-ahead question, you give me a bold-faced lie as an answer, and *you are not even aware at the time that it is a lie.* Because I am the coach, I will stop and pull it out of you and get to the truth. That salesman thing? Get rid of it. Do you remember that I said to you that authenticity and losing the victim stance means you don't want the job, and if you don't want the job, you don't have to sell me anything? With that painted-on smile, you are selling like crazy.

Wayne: That is going to be tough.

Book: You have an opportunity, Wayne.

Wayne: It is not that I don't want to. It is just that I go to motivational seminars where they say if you smile and act happy, you will be happy.

Book: Stop it. Stop going to motivational seminars. Stop it right now. You are not that backward. It is time to get authentic. Remember when you say to me, "That is going to be tough, Stephen," that we are all on your side here. We know how hard that is going to be for you. Keep in mind what English philosopher Edward De Bono says, "That it should be possible to reconsider the efficiency of the wheel." Or, what I read in front of a Unitarian church, "That which does not change is not true."

Wayne: I want to change.

Book: We are going to get a big change out of you, you'll see. This is only the beginning of the interview training. For now, just have the attitude that you are going to meet with me to see if you want to give me the opportunity of representing or casting you. Come in without trying to sell me anything. If you come in honestly looking to see if you are going to give me the opportunity of casting you, why would you spend any time trying to sell me? Do you see how those two attitudes conflict?

Wayne: It was unconscious, though.

Book: I know and now you are becoming conscious. *Self-awareness is the beginning of consciousness*, and with self-awareness may come responsibility for changing.

General Interview Exercise #2 — James

Book: Hi, James. Have a seat.

James: Thanks. You have a poster from the New York Shakespeare Festival.

Book: Yes, I do. Do you like it?

James: Yes, I like it a lot. You have a really big office here.

Book: Yes, it is pretty big. You could park a plane in here.

James: An airplane hanger. That is what I was thinking. You might even be able to do a small shuttle launch.

Book: A little shuttle launch?

James: Park the shuttle, I mean.

Book: I am in the wrong business for that.

James: You have a ballpoint pen in your hand.

Book: I do. I can't remember everybody. I have to take notes.

James: Great. It's impossible to remember everything. It is very conscientious of you.

Book: *Buzz!*

<u>Comments</u>

Book: That was a compliment. He was manipulating me. He was bribing me. He was saying, "I am a caretaker. I can take care of you." Caretakers are very inauthentic and frequently lie. If someone is taking care of you, you dislike it. You feel manipulated. You know that somewhere down the road, the caretaker is going to need something from you, and he is going to expect that you are going to reciprocate and take care of him when he needs you. Caretakers create a unilateral contract between two people.

Who wants to be obligated to a contract that he or she didn't sign? The caretaker's unspoken unilateral contract is, "I'm always going to take care of you. I am going to get you chicken soup. I am going to massage your feet. I am going to be whatever you want me to be, whenever you want me to be there. I am going to do this because somewhere down the line, I am going to need you to be there for me. Because I have been taking care of you for all this time, when that sometime comes in the future, you'll be there for me." Well, that doesn't work because he or she didn't tell you the last part, the *quid pro quo*. Inevitably, that time comes when he or she needs something from you and you don't happen to put as much importance on the moment as the caretaker does. "No, I can't pick you up at the airport at that time—all the rush-hour traffic, and I have a meeting." They feel a massive sense of betrayal with much hurt and anger. You broke the contract! How could you not be there for him or her after all that was done for you? That is the scenario of the caretaker. If you are in any relationship with a caretaker, your body feels something is wrong and it doesn't like it. You are being manipulated. That is what I felt with you when you complimented my note-taking. When you get the opportunity to be on this side of the table, as an interviewer, and you feel that sense of manipulation coming at you, you will stop liking the person.

James: I think it was a form of manipulation, and I agree with what you said about caretaking, but what was happening in my body was I was starting to feel a rapport with you, and for me it was more of a teasing thing than a genuine attempt at bribery.

Book: That rapport that you felt is the goody that comes with telling the first line of truth. Our interview was moving along. Victims have a hard time with success. The minute things start to go well, they are going to go out of their way to screw it up. That's because they are victims, and given how unworthy they think they are, they are not entitled to grow. As we go further into this work we are going to have to pass through a stage where our programmed inauthenticity rebels against our new, burgeoning authenticity. Another way of saying this is, those of you who are inauthentically inclined will go inauthentic at the drop of a hat.

General Interview Exercise #2 — Anthony

Anthony: Hi, Stephen.

Book: Hi.

Anthony: Your desk is a piece of wood on a couple of sawhorses.

Book: I know.

Anthony: (*Sarcastically*) Congratulations. Is this fir? I imagine it is. I assume this is temporary?

Book: *Buzz!*

Comments

Book: The opening truth line was fine. "Your desk is a piece of wood on two sawhorses." I was ready to go with him. Then he started to insult me. He was sarcastic when he said, "Congratulations." Then he said, "I assume this is temporary?" His first line was a perfectly valid statement of truth according to the exercise. Then he beat me up.

General Interview Exercise #2 — Shannon

Shannon: Hi.

Book: Hi.

Shannon: Shannon.

Book: Hi.

Shannon: Pleasure.

Book: Thank you.

Shannon: You have a beautiful, comfortable-looking couch.

Book: Yes.

Shannon: Couches are so important. (*Walking to couch and sitting*) It is very comfortable. It could be very dangerous.

Book: What?

Shannon: I mean, it's so inviting.

Book: Really?

Shannon: It seems to be crying out, "Use me. Use me."

Book: There are a lot of things you can do with a couch.

Shannon: (*Puts her feet up on coffee table*) Mmm.

Book: What else can you do with a couch?

Shannon: I can't think of anything else. Can you?

Book: *Buzz!*

Comments

Book: I feel like she is trying to have sex with me. Reality check: How many of you think the same thing? Shannon, notice that everyone in the room had that same thought. You can't do that. That is big-time manipulation. It is inauthentic and inappropriate to flirt. And if you happen to come across someone who would take you up on it, you will have sex and still not get whatever you want from that person. Or, if the person responds and you back away, you will have turned a contact into an enemy. I support the experimentation of getting out of the chair, but you should be alert about couches. It just sticks out. They don't call it the casting couch for nothing.

General Interview Exercise #2 — Josh

Book: Hello, Josh.

Josh: You have glasses on.

Book: I beg your pardon?

Josh: You have glasses on.

Book: So do you. Actually, they are kind of similar.

Josh: They are kind of shaped the same way. Where did you get yours?

Book: Oliver Peeples.

Josh: Oliver Peeples? Oh, I got mine at Lens Crafters.

Book: Okay.

Josh: *Buzz!* I put down my own glasses. Victim, victim, victim!

Comments

Book: In other words, aren't I a piece of garbage? I shop at Kmart for eyeglasses. Up until there, you were fine, Josh.

General Interview Exercise #2 — Lisa

Lisa: Mr. Book. How are you doing?

Book: Good. How are you?

Lisa: You have a kitchen in your office.

Book: I know.

Lisa: That is so cool.

Book: I know. I wish I could cook.

Lisa: You have two refrigerators.

Book: Actually they are not there.

Lisa: They're not?

Book: It is all done with mirrors.

Lisa: It is all done with mirrors?

Book: I'm kidding.

Lisa: You are kidding. I thought—

Book: It is a temporary space we use for all kinds of stuff. Our other place is so crowded right now that we had to use this space.

Lisa: It is a huge space.

Book: Yes, it is.

Lisa: You are wearing a gray sweater.

Book: I know. It is fantastic. When was the last time you could wear a sweater in this town?

Lisa: I love sweaters. I think I have worn one every day.

Book: Of your life?

Lisa: Of my life. I am very cold-blooded. I just love the feeling of being in a sweater.

Book: You wear sweaters in the middle of the summer?

Lisa: Yes, I do. People think I'm crazy, but I do. Why not?

Book: Whatever.

Lisa: That is a rainbow mug. It reminds me of the Rainbow Coalition. You are probably too young for that. Just kidding.

Book: So—

Lisa: You have a stack of papers there.

Book: Pictures and résumés.

Lisa: Business. Business.

Book: Yes, that is what we do here, business.

Lisa: I have a stapler just like this.

Book: *Buzz!*

Comments

Book: Instead of "I have a stapler just like this," say a truth about that for both of us.

Lisa: The stapler is fuchsia.

Book: Bingo. That would have kept me going. Her saying, "I have a stapler just like this" wouldn't. It is isolated. It is her. If she says, "The stapler is fuchsia-colored," I can see that and am involved. The act of seeing keeps me present *with* her and not isolated, wondering what she expects to gain by telling me she has a similar stapler at home. When we have a common truth between us, we are connected. But she got pretty far.

Follow-Up Questions

How did your interview feel?

Typical answers:

"Better. I had a focus and was more aware of when I was off focus."

"It was free-wheeling and I was not concerned about what happens next."

"I had more of an idea of a goal, and that goal was simply to be truthful. I didn't need his approval."

"It was more interesting."

"I was less vulnerable and more spontaneous."

If your interview lasted for only a few short beats, how did those beats feel?

"It felt good and scary. It felt good because it felt light, and it felt scary because I didn't feel I had any control over it."

"I had a different kind of fear. At first, I felt confident, like 'This is working.' Then I felt, 'Oh my god! Where do I go from here?'"

"It kind of felt like the same feeling you have when you meet someone for the first time and you strike up feelings and you notice something nice just happened. It was then followed by fear of 'now what?'"

"I felt much more interested in what you were saying than in the first round of the exercise."

"I was very calm waiting for my turn because I had the attitude of seeing if I wanted to give you the opportunity of representing me, and then I went out to the bathroom and came back in and was zipping up my fly when you called my turn and I wasn't ready, so I panicked walking up to the desk. I saw my first truth and immediately calmed down."

"I felt involved in an experience."

"I felt like I had you for a second. I feel the same thing in daily life with strangers, like sometimes when they come into the bar where I work and I say, 'What can I get you?' and they just tell you the drink order, and sometimes other people have a little conversation with me and the difference is huge in the pleasure of giving them the drink. And, it has nothing to do with the tipping. I think it has to do with them recognizing that I'm a person and not an object. I understand now that it is important not to make the agent or a casting director an object, and I don't want to make myself an object."

Did you observe differences in one another's interviews from the last interview? What did you see?

"There were fewer questions and answers."

"There was less personal biography and history."

"There was no stuttering and fluttering."

"The interviewer was more involved."

"Each conversation was interesting, engaging, and more fun."

"There was more confidence and energy."

"There was more of everyone's authentic personality."

"There was more connection between the actor and the interviewer."

Summary

For however long these interviews lasted, the actors took responsibility for a victimless and authentic meeting in which the interviewer was relaxed. Soon we will extend those first beats of truthfulness into the whole length of the interview. The actors may not have reached the point where the interviewer had an experience with them, but the kind of foundation that is necessary to build an experience was created.

Truth and experience are two different issues. Don't look for an experience just because there is truth. On the other hand, you can't begin to build an experience without a foundation of truth.

Some common problems with employing the Tell a Truth tool for the first time:

➤ Pre-planning your first line of truth. If you plan ahead, you are moving from the realm of focusing and spontaneity into the realm of manipulation. This is self-defeating. Trust that you can improvise in the moment a single statement of truth. You must trust that you can look out into the room where your meeting is and see or hear something you can point to truthfully.

➤ Looking for a "good" truth line rather than a mundane truth line. The longer you stay in that process of evaluating your truth line, the harder it becomes to discover the first truth line. One truth is as good as another. It is about where the truth leads, not the subject of the first truth. It is all about the experience that has begun when you say a truth to someone who is used to hearing only false statements.

➤ Polluting your truth with a compliment, e.g., "That's a really nice blue sweater you are wearing."

When you say a first truth line, the people you are speaking with might not build upon it. They may simply respond with a simple line like, "Yes, it is." However, that simple line, "Yes, it is," is opening up a channel through which you can send further communication. They are open to receiving communication from you, and that is a strong beginning. Whereas if the first thing you say is inauthentic, the exact opposite will happen—as you know, if anyone has ever tried to pick you up or given you a lot of bullshit for a first line. You put a wall up and shut down. You get angry with them. Don't be distraught if all you get back on their first line is, "Yes, it is." That means that there is an open channel and the ball is in your court to respond with another truth line. It also means that they are willing to listen. You can't ask for more than that when you are meeting strangers.

You noticed that the interviews ended when the natural flow of conversation ended and the agent looked down at your résumé, or when the interviewer felt lied to, manipulated, or was put into the position of being a caretaker. When you feel that happening, especially if you see the interviewer's head start to bend down to your résumé, *tell another truth—or leave. You can choose to end the meeting.* Meetings end when they end. The person who waits to be told when a meeting is over is one-down to the interviewer. Don't be a victim. You can end the meeting instead of giving away that right to the interviewer.

Inauthenticity and the victim stance contribute greatly to keeping struggling actors from making it. There are more than a thousand actors available for every role. Because of those numbers, the business, the industry, can decide that only a few are right. That is why we have the process known as casting.

A common Hollywood story told by successful actors is "I never got anything until I got this confidence, and suddenly I started getting everything." Improving your interview techniques and cleaning up certain issues will result in your building more and more confidence. You can and will turn your victim into a hero.

The Truth-Versus-Compliments-or-Questions Exercise

To understand how a compliment or question undermines your intent to tell a truth, read through this exercise.

Setup

Imagine a person playing the interviewer saying three sets of two lines to you. The first line is a truth, any truth when you and the interviewer face each other. The second line will be either a compliment or a question. Here are pairs of examples.

Set 1:

"That pin on your lapel is a camel. (*Pause*) Why are you
    wearing a camel on your lapel?"

Set 2:

"This is a blue room. (*Pause*) I really like your use of blue."

Set 3:

"Your purse is in your lap." (*Pause*) "Why don't you tie your
    scarf under your lapel—it would enhance your hair style."

Follow-Up Questions

**Do you feel a difference between the two lines in each
set? What does the difference feel like?**

Actor Responding to Set 1: "With the first line you opened
a door and I wanted to respond. The second line put me on the
spot."

Actor Responding to Set 2: "The first line made me smile.
The second line made me defensive."

Actor Responding to Set 3: "With the first line I felt
trusting and with the second I felt manipulated, embarrassed,
and wary."

The response to the first line will always be positive; the response
to the second line will always be negative and could include feelings
of being violated, invaded, or made to feel dirty.

Summary

The first line was a straight-ahead statement of truth, and everyone had a perfectly natural, relaxed, comfortable feeling when
the line was spoken. Everything was fine until the second line was
spoken. The second line was simply a compliment or question, but

the actors had negative reactions. The lesson to be learned here is don't turn your truth statement into a compliment, e.g., "this is a brown chair" versus "this is an interesting brown chair." Compliments not only manipulate the one to whom you are talking, they also enslave you. After you pay a compliment, you feel that you have to justify the compliment in some way. Remove the compliment and feel freer.

Even when the second line is spoken in a neutral fashion without any attitude, a compliment or question will carry an implication of attitude. Attitude always accompanies a compliment. This is especially true in a business meeting. It may be different in a personal relationship. It is probably very authentic to turn to your lover and say, "Wow, that is a gorgeous sweater you have on." But in a business situation, you are going to get negative reactions. Do this exercise with a friend and experientially learn how you feel comfortable when being told a simple statement of truth compared to the feelings of unease when you are complimented or questioned.

3

Building an Experience

"Avoid I" Exercise

"**A**void I" is an exercise for discovering and developing ideas and heightening the communication of them. Both of these components will extend your ability to create an experience. Although this exercise is written for pairs of people, the lessons it teaches are available to the single reader, who may practice the focus of this exercise in any social situation.

Setup

Select a topic for a five-minute conversation. Choosing the topic is not part of the conversation. During the conversation you are to *avoid saying the word* "I" and *avoid asking questions*. You are to share the conversation, and you are not allowed to bypass the rules with cleverness. In other words, you can't substitute for *I* the royal *we*, the universal *you*, or the word *one*, as in "one might go to the movies." You also must avoid questions, conceptually as well as literally. Sharing the conversation means that both of you will speak freely and easily without one doing all the talking and the other doing all the listening.

Rules and Focus

Avoid saying the word *I*. Avoid questions.

Follow-Up Questions

Were you able to avoid the word *I*?

Did you ask questions?

What did you notice about yourself during this conversation?

Was there a change in your conversation as a result of following the rules?

Did you discover anything else?

Did you discover anything about yourself—how you speak or what you say?

Did you discover anything about your partner?

Was anything different about this conversation from your normal conversations?

How did that make you feel?

Summary

When you are on your focus, you will experience the joy of discovering new ideas with heightened energy, and that will lead to heightened communication. This will be a step forward in the direction of transforming any conversation into an experience. Remember that you may practice this focus in any social situation without telling anyone what you are doing.

The actors who practiced this in a group situation responded that their conversations became more about the subject and what was going on between them and less about themselves. Their interest in the subject or topic, regardless of how it changed, was piqued, and they explored it further than they normally would have. They found that their brains worked faster and were more focused:

"I felt that my brain worked a little freer, that I was a little more in that freewheeling space where my brain was ahead of what I was saying, rather than a position of just kind of speaking to speak. When I spoke, my thoughts had become full sentences with greater clarity and deeper meaning. While everything I said was more purposeful, there were no feelings of labor or effort. While I took more time to formulate what I was thinking and saying it didn't really slow the conversation down." For another, "Ordinarily when I speak, th-there—I—I—I—th-th-th-the—and—ye-ye-ye (*continues stammering*), and that didn't happen. Normally I start speaking faster than I'm thinking, and then there's a lag between—I—I've started a sentence and there's no longer a thought to finish it. I've got to stall, in my case through stammering, until that thought catches up with my words. That stalling and stammering disappeared!"

They also noticed they had more interest and were more invested in their partner's contribution to the conversation. "I felt like the topic was something between us, that we were each throwing things in and taking things out. I was listening, but not waiting for him.

The two of us were making a big salad, and we just couldn't wait to put more ingredients into it." The actors also discovered that they were omitting personal anecdotes related to past events in their lives. When their conversation partners omitted personal anecdotes, the actors were put more on the hook or edge. When a person tells an anecdote it buys time for the listener to retreat out of the communication experience and into his or her own head, where he or she can think about what to say next. Without anecdotes, you have no down time, and you cannot remove yourself from the communication experience.

You will find that you actually become smarter as you discover purpose and meaning in your conversations. You're not just speaking to fill time. Instead, you are forced to examine your topic, and you begin seeing the significance of it. Discovering or seeing the significance helps you to create new thoughts and ideas, ones you want to share because it is exciting. This creates a heightened energy flow *between* you, which in an interview will translate as an experience.

When you use the word *I*, you tend to tell stories you already know. "Last night *I* did this, *I* did that." It creates isolation. There is no adventure and no spontaneity because you are following the script of your story. When you don't use the word *I*, you are more open to having an adventure, going somewhere new. You're on a journey of thoughts. Get rid of the word *I* and go exploring. Find out what is going on between you and another person.

Questions should be avoided because they interrupt the evolving flow of conversational energy. Asking questions, even if the questions pertain to the subject, will likely dampen the charge that is building between the two of you because the other person will have to stop being with you (in the experience) and go into his or her head (in isolation) to answer the question.

With the Avoid I exercise, you experienced or learned about a new kind of conversation, which is one kind of an experience. In order to have a sense of what another kind of experience feels like, *Yes! And . . .* is an improv you can do, or read about, or even practice the next time you participate in any group discussion.

Yes! And . . .[1]

Setup

Select a type of committee that is planning an event or marketing a product, such as a PTA rummage sale. Your team, composed of from two to five members, will place chairs in a semi-circle. Each time each member speaks he or she has to begin with, "Yes! And . . ." The improv should last about five minutes. If you do not have people to work with, please practice Yes! And . . . the next time you have a conversation with anyone.

Rules and Acting Focus

Everyone must remain seated and take equal responsibility for sharing the discussion. All dialogue must begin with the two words *Yes! And . . .*, and you must build on each other's words and enthusiasm.

Follow-Up Questions

Did you share the conversation?

Did you begin your lines with the words *Yes! And . . .*?

Were you on focus?

Did you dive in or were you hesitant?

Were you enthusiastic?

Did you build on each other's enthusiasm?

What were some of the feelings you experienced playing Yes! And . . .?

Summary

Because of the *and*, you were always adding something new to the improvisation and extending it. It was never just an echo of what had been previously stated. You felt as if you were part of a conversation that was continually building. With this exercise you should have experienced authentic feelings of enthusiasm and excitement. What were some of the feelings you experienced when playing Yes! And . . .? You must have felt as if you were part of something that was building. You probably felt light, carefree, involved, inventive, enthusiastic, engaged, exhilarated, charged, excited, inspired, edge-of-your-seat fearless, and totally focused on what was being said. All of these responses are common to many types of experiences with an interviewer. Whatever your feelings were, notice that they were related to what was happening *between* you and your conversational partner(s) in the present tense. Heightened feelings arising from what is happening between you in the present tense is a prerequisite for any kind of an experience. There are different variations of this kind of experience, and we will get to them.

In order to have a positive experience with another person, you must respect the other person. This respect begins with devoting your full attention to the other person, seeing and hearing him or her. Reflection, an acting focus used in theater games and Improvisation Technique, will introduce you to the "body feelings," which accompany your giving "full body" respect to another person. In this section on Basic Reflection and the next on Reflection Listening you will benefit from reading them, but you will understand them better if a friend does the exercises with you.

Basic Reflection[2]

Setup

Each of you is assigned the number one or the number two. Face each other with about four feet between you. If only two of you are doing the exercise, read the rules first to understand the exercise and take turns calling out the switches.

Rules

One actor will *reflect* the movements and expressions of the other actor, mirroring the other person head to toe. In each pair, one player will initiate movement, and the other player will reflect what he or she sees. Begin with the "ones" initiating and the "twos" reflecting. The initiators can make any kind of movement, but it has to be done without taking steps. They can make facial expressions, can move their bodies in an abstract manner, can use "space props" (e.g., space guitar), or do a little activity (e.g., brushing teeth with a space toothbrush)—anything without taking steps. If you are the initiator, help the reflector—this is not about tricking your partner. The two of you are working together as a team to achieve a complete and total reflection with no lag in time. Initiators, you should never come to a stop—one movement should flow into the next. Reflectors, focus on complete and total reflection. Facial expressions reflect facial expressions; hands reflect hands; knees reflect knees. Reflect everything you see, not what you want to see or what you anticipate seeing.

After about a minute, switch roles without stopping the movement. Let the movement continue as the "twos" take on the role of initiator and the "ones" reflect. You needn't come to a stop; in fact, you don't want to stop the game and start anew. If you are the new initiator you may take the movement wherever you want. Keep the movement fluid. Avoid coming to a stop. Initiate anything you wish—explore new kinds of movement. If you are the new mirror, reflect everything that you see—elbows, faces, knees, etcetera. Work together, but in complete silence.

Switch again. Without hesitating or stopping, change roles. The "ones" become the initiators; the "twos," reflectors. You are working together to create a mirror effect. Initiators, never come to a stop.

Switch again. Initiators, keep the movement fluid. Avoid coming to a stop. Let each movement transform into the next. Switch. Whether you're initiating or reflecting, stay on focus. I recommend staying on your feet. Don't sit or kneel. Repeat switches at varied intervals. Always know if you are initiating or reflecting. The entire playing time should be about seven minutes.

If an extra person is available, he or she can coach the rules and call out the switches as needed.

Acting Focus

For the reflector, you are to reflect what you see; for the initiator, you are to initiate movement for your partner to reflect.

Follow-Up Questions

Were you on the acting focus?

Did you reflect what you saw as you saw it, or did you reflect what you anticipated seeing?

When you were initiating, did you keep the movement flowing?

Continue with the next exercise. Again you will benefit from reading the exercise, but you will gain more if you practice the exercise with a friend.

Reflection Listening[3]

Setup

Pair up in teams of two and sit facing each other on chairs or on the floor. Take a minute to select a topic for conversation. Choosing the topic is not part of the conversation. Avoid trivial topics; select instead a topic that will form the basis for a real conversation.

Part One

Rules

Here are the two main guidelines for your conversation: practice avoiding the word *I*, and also avoid asking questions. You are not being told not to use questions or the word *I* but to avoid them. If you do ask a question or use the word *I*, your partner should not call attention to it. If you are aware of your asking a question or using the word *I*, try not to do it again. Don't put yourself down if you don't always succeed in accomplishing your goals. In Part One, all you are to do is have a spontaneous conversation with your partner. You have chosen a topic and you should allow the conversation to evolve.

Acting Focus

When your partner is speaking, you are to focus on *reflecting your partner's lips*. This is a two-sided conversation, and while one person is speaking, the other person is listening and reflecting the speaker's lips. Whenever the speaking role switches, so does the listening/reflecting role. In order to create the reflection, you have to be looking at the lips. You are not reflecting the other's face; you are reflecting the lips. Your lips should be moving without sound, forming the same words your partner is saying as closely as possible to the same time as he or she is saying them. *Do not change the rules of the exercise for any reason.* Look at the speaker's lips and reflect the speaker's lips. You want the briefest possible lag time between the speaking and the reflecting. The speaking partner should speak normally and not slow his or her speech down. When speaking, it is not necessary to look at the listener's lips. Continue the conversation for five to ten minutes, speaking and listening to each other. When you are the listener, reflect the speaker's lips. There are to be no comments about the acting focus itself.

Part Two

Acting Focus

Now stop. You will get to continue these conversations in a minute. You have to revise your focus in order to move on to Part Two, which is the main level of the exercise. Let's review what has been happening here. If you are silent and not talking, you are creating no energy. But when you start speaking, you do create energy. When your partner reflects you, he or she is taking in this energy in two ways. First, your partner is listening to your words and, as a result, is hearing. The energy is moving from you, the speaker, in through the listener's ears. Second, the listener's eyes are on your mouth, so there is a second path of energy flowing from the speaker's mouth into the listener's eyes. The listener, who is creating no energy, is receiving two paths of energy: through the ears and through the eyes. These two paths of energy merge inside the listener, and then they are expressed back out into the space through the listener's moving lips. The listener is now creating more energy than he or she would by just listening. This is what you have done.

In Part Two, you play almost the same way as in Part One. You still listen to the speaker's words. You still keep your eyes on the speaker's lips. You still receive the two paths of energy from the speaker's mouth and words. You still let those energy paths merge inside you, and right at the moment when that energy is about to be expressed back out into the space through your lips moving, *stop moving your lips*. You should feel exactly as you did when your lips were moving; but at the moment when you would move your lips in a reflection response, don't. It is essentially the same process, only you are not to move your lips. This acting focus is called *Reflection Listening*.

This is the focus for Part Two. Commit to the focus and do *not come up with any reason whatsoever to improve on it*. Don't change the rules. Keep your eyes glued to the lips of the speaker and your ears to the words of the speaker. When you resume, pick up your conversation where you left off. Avoid using *I* and avoid asking questions if you can. Don't move your lips. The speaking partner should speak normally, not slower than usual. When speaking, it is not necessary to look at the listener's lips. When you speak, your partner is to participate by using Reflection Listening. Then that partner will reply to what is said and you become the reflection listener. *Go right back into your conversations and stay on this acting focus*. Continue the conversation for five to ten minutes, speaking and Reflection Listening to each other. If you have difficulty understanding the focus for Part Two, have your partner or a third person read the Part Two: Acting Focus paragraphs out loud to you while you reflect his or her lips as in Part One. At the appropriate moment in the second paragraph, follow the instructions and stop moving your lips.

Follow-Up Questions

Were you able to maintain communication? You will probably answer yes.

Was the *quality* of your conversation the same as that of your usual conversations?

Or was it heightened or lessened? You will probably agree that it was heightened.

What was different about these conversations from your normal conversations?

What did you notice about your own physical being during these conversations?

Did you notice you were leaning in toward your partner?

Did you have any kind of experience?

Was it different from the experience you had playing Yes! And . . .?

Summary

You should agree that the quality of your conversation was better than normal and that you were intensely involved with your partner. You must also have noticed that you were *leaning in*. You involved your body physiologically in the *listening* process. You were totally involved in the present tense with each other. That's what the leaning in was all about.

In the Now

The "body feeling" you experienced in this exercise is the feeling that comes with your being in the moment and focused on the here and now. You didn't run an inner monologue commenting on the other person while he or she spoke. You didn't judge another human being in the process. You didn't finish anybody else's sentences the way you frequently do in normal conversation. You allowed the person to finish his or her own sentences. You didn't plan your own sentences ahead of time, nor did you feel the need to do so. You brought your body to every word as it was said to you. That's called being *in the now*, or in the moment. It's called spontaneous listening and speaking. Both parties in the same present-tense moment at the same time, ready to go wherever the conversation leads. You are in a state of waiting in readiness, which is an essential feature of being in the now.

Respect

The single word that should describe your experience playing Reflection Listening is *respect*. Every moment that you're playing Reflection Listening is a moment of heightened respect for the other person. You are giving your entire being to the other person without distraction, without judgment, without editorializing, without commentary, and without inauthenticity. This is utter respect.

Reflecting Lips Versus Looking at Eyes

In reflection listening, you have to look at the speaker's lips in order to reflect his or her words. For some of you, this may create a dilemma because you feel that it's important to look in the other person's *eyes*.

I suggest that most of the time when you choose to look into the eyes of someone who's talking to you, you have a hidden agenda. Let's say you meet someone and you're attracted to this person. Usually you will look the person in the eyes while he or she is talking. The hidden agenda, a form of manipulation, is letting that person know what a sincere and terrific person you are, which has nothing to do with the topic of conversation or the process of communicating. Also, when you look into the person's eyes, you tend to go into your head and have an inner monologue, commenting on the other person or on what is being said instead of having authentic, spontaneous communication. Instead of being in the now you focus on what you want to read into the other person. You impose your story on him or her. That can be adventurous, fun, and romantic or it can be judgmental, dangerous, and objectifying, but it is *not* about communication or what is happening *between* you and your partner.

What you found with Reflection Listening is that your partner's lips are so active compared to the eyes that your involvement in reflecting the movement of the lips takes you out of your hidden agendas, inner monologues, judgments, and future-tense thinking and planning. You're so busy *doing* something that you get out of your own way. The result is *authentic communication*.

Demonstration

There is a difference between looking at someone's lips and Reflection Listening. Try a demonstration so that you can *understand* the difference. Return to conversing with your partner for one minute. Get off the acting focus. Instead, look at your partner's lips, but don't play Reflection Listening. Just look at your partner's lips. You should feel something very different from what you felt in Reflection Listening. Do you see how you've gone off? Your mind is wandering. All you're doing is displaying superficial attentiveness. That is *not* the acting focus of Reflection Listening. Looking at people's lips is *not* what you've been practicing.

Now, continue the conversation for another minute and return to playing Reflection Listening. Do you feel the difference? When you are just looking at your partner's lips, your mind wanders—you become distracted and self-conscious. If you are truly playing Reflection Listening, your mind *can't* wander. You are too busy to be distracted or to become self-conscious.

Should there be any confusion about the difference between looking in the other's eyes versus playing reflection speech, repeat the above demonstration and for *looking at the lips*, substitute: "And, instead, look at the eyes. Don't play Reflection Listening. Just look in your partner's eyes."

Is It Noticeable?

When you focus on Reflection Listening will the other person notice you are looking at his or her mouth? The people who will notice a difference are the ones with whom you already have close relationships because they are used to your behaving one way:

"Why are you so focused and attentive?" they'll ask. However, if you focus on Reflection Listening with people who don't know you well, they will be so caught up in your respect for them that they will not notice you focusing on a particular part of their faces. Experiment with Reflection Listening in social situations until you feel comfortable doing it and have proven to yourself that no one is thinking about where you are looking.

General Interview Exercise #3

Setup

It is possible to just read through this exercise to benefit from its lessons, but, as always, it may be better to participate in it with a friend. One of you plays the role of the interviewer and interviews the other actor. Then you reverse roles and conduct another interview. Each actor, therefore, participates in two interviews: one as himself and one as an interviewer. The interviewer this time is playing the role of a network casting director, who has a copy of the actor's picture and résumé. The actor playing the casting director conducts the interview according to his or her interviewing experiences in similar situations. The interview begins when the casting director calls out the actor's name, and when the casting director feels that the conversation has ended, she or he may thank the actor for coming in and end the interview.

Use the Tools

When you are being interviewed, practice the tools with which you have been working.

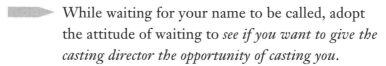 While waiting for your name to be called, adopt the attitude of waiting to *see if you want to give the casting director the opportunity of casting you.*

> During the meeting adopt the attitude that *you don't want anything from the interviewer*. It follows that if you don't want anything, *you don't have to sell anything*.

> When your meeting starts—as soon as you say hello—*tell a truth* about what you see or hear in the office.

> When the initial conversation, which flows from your first truth line, starts to fade, *tell another truth*.

In addition, be open to employing your new tools from this chapter.

> After the conversation gets rolling, choose to employ the acting focus, Reflection Listening. Do not use this acting focus if the conversation isn't rolling along. If your "telling a truth" line gets a conversation started, experiment with Reflection Listening. Also experiment with Reflection Listening if you find yourself nervous, inauthentic, or bored.

> At any time during the conversation you can give it an energy boost by playing Yes! And . . .

> When you feel you have made your impact, *end the conversation*.

If you are playing the casting director and recognize that the person you are interviewing is doing Reflection Listening, go with whatever is happening between you, but do not play Reflection Listening yourself because no interviewer would ever do it. You should end the interview if the conversation has stopped flowing and there is a lull or if you feel you are being manipulated.

Workshop Actors' Interviews

General Interview Exercise #3 — Josh

Josh: How are you doing?

Casting Director: Good. How are you?

Josh: Good.

Casting Director: Thanks for coming in.

Josh: You are wearing blue jeans.

Casting Director: Yes. They are comfortable. Long day at the office. It is good to be comfortable.

Josh: Yes, it is good to be comfortable. You are wearing a leather jacket.

Casting Director: Yes. It is cold outside. I can't seem to get warm. Are you warm?

Josh: I am warm. I have wool socks on. I am wearing a jacket. You have a purple shirt on underneath that.

Casting Director: Yes. It is like long underwear. I get really cold.

Josh: You are wearing long underwear.

Casting Director: Just the top. I left the bottoms at home. It is a big space; it is hard to keep warm.

Josh: It is a big space.

Casting Director: Yes it is.

Josh: You could put a lot of stuff in this space.

Casting Director: Yes.

Josh: You could park a car in this space.

Casting Director: Two cars.

Josh: Yes! And a truck. A plane. A trailer. A horse and trailer. Horses. You could keep horses in here. They don't make too much noise.

Casting Director: Could be messy.

Josh: Newspaper. You could just put newspaper down underneath. You could train horses in here.

Casting Director: You could.

Josh: You could be The Horse Whisperer. You wouldn't have to make a lot of noise. You could do it very quietly.

Casting Director: In this big a space, I wouldn't have to whisper. I could scream. Hey!

Josh: We could scream. Hey!

Casting Director: You have a nice voice. Have you had a lot of training?

Josh: Thank you. I have had some training. Mostly just talking.

Casting Director: That is good training, I guess.

Josh: You are not wearing a watch.

Casting Director: I am, actually. (*Pulls sleeve back*)

Josh: It is a Conan watch.

Casting Director: Iron Man.

Josh: Oh, Iron Man.

Casting Director: I'm not an iron man. I just feel like I am with the watch.

Josh: Very few of us actually are, you know, iron men.

Casting Director: That's true.

Josh: They work underwater. Those watches.

Casting Director: It works in the shower. I never take it off.

Josh: You have a homemade desk.

Casting Director: It is temporary. The rooms are in the process of being redecorated. We are getting new furniture in the next few weeks. Just using this stuff for the interviews we are doing this week. What have you been doing lately?

Josh: Me? I have been going to the gym; doing a little bit of exercising.

Casting Director: Which gym?

Josh: The Crunch Gym, the one by Sunset Park.

Casting Director: You like that?

Josh: Yes, I do. You ever go to the movies there?

Casting Director: No. I live on the west side, so not usually. I go to Santa Monica.

Josh: There is a movie theater down there on Second Street, I think. They show a lot of independent films there.

Casting Director: Yes.

Josh: That movie, *Sideways*, is playing at the $2.50 movie theater.

Casting Director: Yes. It is great. I have seen it.

Josh: You have seen it? I just like paying $2.50.

Casting Director: Better than a matinee.

Josh: Better than a matinee. (*Pause*) Well, it has been nice meeting you.

Casting Director: And nice meeting you, too.

Josh: So long.

Casting Director: Thanks very much, Josh, for coming in.

General Interview Exercise #3 — Anthony

Anthony: Hi.

Casting Director: Hi.

Anthony: How are you?

Casting Director: Fine. How are you?

Anthony: Fine. Thanks. There is a small coffee table over there with a red clock on it.

Casting Director: Yes, there is. It is kind of burgundy.

Anthony: A little lighter than my sweater.

Casting Director: Yes.

Anthony: There is a rolling cart with a whole lot of photography supplies on it.

Casting Director: Yes, it looks like some kind of craft center.

Anthony: You do the arts and crafts in here then?

Casting Director: Yes, on roller-skates.

Anthony: Wow! That would be fun. That would be dangerous and fun.

Casting Director: Yes.

Anthony: With that spotlight, you can see who you are hitting.

Casting Director: It is sort of like The Roxy.

Anthony: Yes.

Casting Director: Arts and crafts on wheels.

Anthony: Yes. Sort of like being at one of those drive-in places with waitresses on wheels and roller-skates.

Casting Director: Not a bad idea, actually.

Anthony: They don't do it anymore . . . only at Bob's in Burbank.

Casting Director: I don't know it.

Anthony: It is on Riverside in Burbank.

Casting Director: It is what, a restaurant?

Anthony: Yes, Bob's Big Boy, the statue out front of the big, fat guy with the checked overalls, the big, fat guy with the big head of hair.

Casting Director: I'll have to go by sometime.

Anthony: That statue just screams, "Good food!" doesn't it?

Casting Director: It could.

Anthony: There is a loft area up there.

Casting Director: Yes, there is. We store stuff up there.

Anthony: You put the snowman up there. (*Pointing to a big cardboard snowman*)

Casting Director: Someone put the snowman up there.

Anthony: It reminds me of Christmas—wintertime.

Casting Director: It reminds you of Christmas?

Anthony: Yes. Snowmen, they remind me of wintertime.

Casting Director: You are not from L.A.?

Anthony: No. I am from Chicago. It still feels like Christmastime, though, especially when there are snowmen in the loft.

Casting Director: Either that or a horror flick.

Anthony: Yes. Beware of the snowman from the loft! He pulls out his carrot nose and lunges at you. He could have used those ladders to climb up there.

Casting Director: Frosty?

Anthony: Yes. Beware of the snowman going up the ladder into the loft.

Casting Director: With his carrot knife.

Anthony: Right. He's coming to get ya.

Casting Director: Me?

Anthony: (*Whispering*) I'm just warning everybody.

Casting Director: We are the only ones here.

Anthony: As far as we know. There is no one under the desk.

Casting Director: There is no one under the desk. Very astute observation.

Anthony: I've been trained to observe . . . under desks. Well, thanks for having me in.

Casting Director: Thanks for coming by.

Anthony: Have a nice day.

General Interview Exercise #3 — Lisa

Lisa: How you doing?

Casting Director: Hi, Lisa. Nice to meet you.

Lisa: Nice to meet you, too. You have polo on your sweatshirt.

Casting Director: Oh, yes. You know, Ralph Lauren preppy stuff.

Lisa: It is not an alligator, though.

Casting Director: It is not an alligator.

Lisa: But they are both preppy, aren't they?

Casting Director: I believe they are.

Lisa: I don't know which is more preppy.

Casting Director: I like Ralph better than the alligators.

Lisa: It is very white, but it is a winter white.

Casting Director: Yes, it is kind of an off-white.

Lisa: You have your glasses around your neck.

Casting Director: Yes, I have to keep them within easy reach so I can get to them.

Lisa: You have to be able to see.

Casting Director: I have to be able to see, and I don't like to have to go looking for glasses.

Lisa: Especially when you can't see.

Casting Director: Especially when I can't see, I can't find them.

Lisa: That would be a hard thing. I actually had that problem recently, so I can relate.

Casting Director: You wear glasses?

Lisa: I am just a little bit near-sighted.

Casting Director: I am near-sighted, too.

Lisa: If you were far-sighted, you would probably be wearing glasses to see résumés.

Casting Director: Exactly.

Lisa: I guess I could have guessed that. You also have your collar buttoned down there.

Casting Director: I guess I am preppy today, aren't I?

Lisa: You have mastered the look, yes.

Casting Director: I don't know if I like that.

Lisa: Well—

Casting Director: It's just that you brought it up.

Lisa: I did bring it up. You are right about that.

Casting Director: It is just a habit.

Lisa: (*Pointing to makshift desk*) There is blue there, there, there, and there.

Casting Director: Yes, we have seemed to cover some spaces on it, haven't we?

Lisa: A couple. Not too many, though, actually. It is actually very intermittent.

Casting Director: Very spontaneous.

Lisa: It seems spontaneous. I don't know how anyone could have done that intentionally.

Casting Director: It was probably used in the prop department to paint something.

Lisa: Yes. That makes sense. So, I must run. Thank you for meeting with me.

Casting Director: The pleasure was all mine.

General Interview Exercise #3 — Shannon

Shannon: Hi.

Casting Director: Hi. Nice to meet you, Shannon.

Shannon: Nice to meet you.

Casting Director: Have a seat.

Shannon: Look at that whole little area, a whole little living room.

Casting Director: Yes. It is a little makeshift thing we have going on.

Shannon: You could sleep on that couch. It is a very long couch.

Casting Director: It comes in handy for naps.

Shannon: Sleeping on the job, huh?

Casting Director: Just little catnaps.

Shannon: I couldn't have a couch in my office, or I might take more than one or two catnaps on it. I can't even have a very comfortable chair. The walls are freshly painted.

Casting Director: They are freshly painted.

Shannon: Yes! And they look like white canvases.

Casting Director: Yes, they do. We are just setting up here.

Shannon: They almost cry out for children with finger-paints to come by and smear all over them.

Casting Director: Well, sometimes we do have children around here. They are my colleagues' kids.

Shannon: You better keep an eye on them if you want to keep your white walls. My goodness that is a small stapler.

Casting Director: Yes.

Shannon: And pink, hot pink. I guess that doesn't hold a lot of staples?

Casting Director: No, it doesn't. Maybe ten or so.

Shannon: It is really huge in here.

Casting Director: It is huge. I like it. I am used to really small spaces. This is a nice change.

Shannon: Your voice can bounce off the ceiling.

Casting Director: There is a kind of an echo, isn't there?

Shannon: (*Sings out a loud musical note*) Sorry. I have very big ceilings in my house, and I used to always notice the echo. After a while, you get used to it and you don't notice it.

Casting Director: It gets very chilly.

Shannon: It is very chilly outside. I hope it doesn't last very long.

Casting Director: Our winter is definitely beginning.

Shannon: I never remember it getting this cold before. This doesn't seem like a normal L.A. winter.

Casting Director: It can get cold.

Shannon: I know, it must have something to do with the cheese, based on those billboards.

Casting Director: The cheese? I haven't heard about that.

Shannon: Those billboards . . . they are all over L.A. They say El Niño keeps coming back because of the cheese. I knew what the cheese ads were before I knew what El Niño was. I just knew that El Niño meant "the child" in Spanish, and I just didn't get it. "The child . . . ," that is why all these people are eating cheese? I wasn't educated enough to get it. Now I know all about Los Angeles cheese. (*Rising*) Hey, it's been great to meet you.

Casting Director: Yes, it has. I'm glad you came in.

Shannon: Bye.

Follow-Up Questions

Did you start with a truth?

If it were necessary, did you tell another truth?

Did you use Reflection Listening?

If you were able to employ Reflection Listening, think about or share your experiences.

Did you use Yes! And . . . ? Share your experiences of that.

Did you end the meeting when it was ended?

Did you notice a big difference in your interviews from the first round?

Typical Responses from the Actors

James: Reflection Listening made me aware of when I was losing the truth. It gave me more of a cue and time to jump in with something. It relieved tension.

Dorian: I found it very grounding. When I felt a little scattered, I would go back to it.

Josh: I was using Reflection Listening, and when the interviewer stopped talking, I didn't feel a little bit of panic like, "Oh my God, I have to say something." There was less pressure.

Brian: I felt my senses increase. My hearing was better and more acute, and everything around me seemed heightened.

Lisa: Listening and reacting was much easier.

Anthony: It felt like when we improvise—it was very in the moment.

Shannon: I think I was less aware of how I was being perceived, because when I look in someone's eyes, I frequently see a reflection of myself. This time I reflected Tracy's lips, and that was so much more personal about her, not me. It made me more aware of her and what she was talking about rather than looking for approval from her.

Wayne: The first few times I applied the Reflection Listening I felt really uncomfortable with it, but as it went on, it took away any kind of nervousness that would try to creep up.

Tracy: The casting director seemed to talk more. The casting director or interviewer seemed to talk more about himself.

The most common responses were that the people being interviewed felt less panicky and more connected. They said it helped them listen and spend less time thinking about what to say next. They felt more spontaneous.

What did you discover by playing the role of the interviewer?

People usually answer that they felt the actor wanted to hear what the interviewer had to say, and that drew the interviewer in. That feeling of *being drawn in is the beginning of the interviewer having an experience.*

Typical Responses from the Interviewers

Mark: I felt a sense of relief when I heard something that was obviously true.

Wayne: I kept wanting to go to the résumé and see what she had done. I felt that, at some point, I was going to have to do that, but she kept taking my attention back to her, and I felt very good about it.

Christina: There was no stress on me when I was playing the interviewer, and it was really easy to kick back. Also, I began to really see how it feels when there is a lull, how put upon you feel and when the actor jumps in there how much better it feels.

Josh: I felt almost relief when I saw how stressful it is to be an interviewer, because when there was a lull, I found myself thinking, "What the hell am I going to say? Am I going to sit here and stare at this person?" Even going to the résumé, I felt a lot of pressure, and before I had no idea what they felt like when you go in there.

Summary

Reflection Listening

Using Reflection Listening allows you to begin to create an experience with the interviewer because it brings you together in the present tense. Additionally there's no time left to go into your victim stance or perform inauthentically. Reflection Listening transcends those behaviors and makes you present in the moment.

It's like acting. Acting is doing—and there's always more to do. One of the benefits of *doing* in acting is that your mind is so involved in the *doing* that it doesn't have time to get itself in trouble, or what we call being "in the head." That process is now brought to the interview. Interviewing is also *doing*, and there's always more to do. The equivalent of being "in the head" in an interview is lying, manipulating, and assuming a victim stance, all of which make the interviewer want to get you out of the office at once.

Telling a Truth

Avoid using the same exact word phrase in every truth line. If all of your truth lines start with, "You have a. . . ," they may be too notice-

able. Mix them up, i.e., "That is a . . ."; "There is the . . ."; "This is a
. . ."; "Here is a . . .." Make sure that every one of your truth lines is
a full declarative sentence. Telling your truth in a sentence fragment
will make the interviewer think that you are a victim or a fool.

Every time you tell a truth you will relieve the interviewer of the
responsibility of taking care of you and surprise him or her with
your lack of manipulation. The energy surrounding a surprise is
the same energy that accompanies an experience.

The ultimate interview will not look like these interviews with
five, six, or seven truth lines. When we are finished with this training process, you will start your interviews with one truth line to
establish authenticity, and then you'll move on to the experience.
In this round of interviews we were practicing how to achieve immediate authenticity and rapport. In the future, you will probably
only need to tell a truth at the first moment of the interview and
then you will be able to focus on building the experience. Telling a
truth is an important tool for creating the foundation upon which
to create an experience. Telling a truth makes the other person
comfortable, and people have to be comfortable with each other
before they can have a good time.

When you did your first interviews you were negative in your
approaches. In this round you were neutral. You are now able to
participate in an interview without assuming a victim stance or acting in an inauthentic manner. You are now clean, fresh, and neutral,
and you have made a solid foundation for building an experience.
In the next chapter, we will build on this foundation and learn how
to heighten the experience for you and the interviewer and how to
take your transformation from neutral to positive.

Career Applications

Book: Let's check in. Has anybody had the opportunity to employ any of the new tools in a career situation since the last class?

Andrew: I had two interviews: One was with a casting director and one was with a manager. At the first one, the guy was Irish and I'm Scotch/Irish, so I used that as a truth topic. We quickly got around to talking about whiskey. We laughed about Scotland. I chose to end the meeting, got up and shook the guy's hand, and walked out. The next day they called me back for an audition. Then I went in to meet a manager, a lady, and I did the same thing. I went in, shook hands, and there was a picture of Marilyn Monroe behind the lady's head, and that was what I pointed out with my truth line. We got into this whole conversation and it went on and on and it went great. We laughed a lot. I got up to leave and she said, "Sit down." I sat down and we talked for another twenty minutes and I said, "Well, okay, I gotta get—" And she said, "Oh come on, sit down." Kept me there an hour, but I now have a manager.

Laura: I went into an agency and I wasn't nervous to meet with the first guy because he was young and whatever. I passed that part, so he brought me in to meet the head of the agency, and I took one look at her and knew she was going to be a real tough cookie. I walked into the office and looked at the bulletin board behind her, and there was a poster of an actor who is actually the father of a friend of mine, so it struck me right away, and I just said, "You have a picture of 'so and so' on your wall." We started a whole conversation about him, and it turned out that he was invited to a party she had planned for her husband, and she went into this whole thing about her husband. It was great. We completely connected on that, and it softened her up right away, and they want to sign me.

Mark: I had an audition. I was in the room with three other actors, and I wanted to just watch everybody else, just to see what was going on, and it was amazing. All of them, except one who was a real experienced actor, were doing a victim stance. One guy was walking around the room trying to chat everyone up. One guy was in the corner trying to start conversations with complaints like, "What a hell of a time to have an audition!" A lot of the things he was doing were creating a victim of himself. In watching that, in being aware of what was going on, I was able to stay focused on what I had to do when I went in to audition.

Dorian: It was kind of a weird thing. I went in to meet a casting director, and she pulled it on me. She said, "You are wearing black." It freaked me out for a second, and then I gave it right back with, "You are wearing a sweatshirt." It totally took me back that she did that. Then I had this other situation. Someone told me about an audition, and I just sort of ran over there to see if they would let me in. Instead of begging, I took on the attitude of "taking the opportunity to see if I wanted to let them cast me." They let me audition even though I didn't have an appointment. It went really well.

James: I have had several commercial auditions in the last week, and each time I went in with the intention of telling a truth. Just doing the process of being engaged and looking for something to tell a truth about had a very centering effect. And, like Dorian said, I actually had someone start off a conversation with me by stating a truth. My reaction was very pleasant. It was like, "Oh, yes," and it all returned and it felt very nice. It created much less of the nervous wanting thing that I sometimes feel. Sometimes to avoid that in the past, I have retreated into a "professional stoic" kind of thing. I find this more engaging, just to be looking out for something to tell a truth about, than pretending to be a cool professional.

Brian: I had an opportunity to substitute for my friend as a reader at a casting session for a feature film. It was really insightful to see in action what we are working on. So many actors come in and just kill themselves—just shoot themselves in the foot. I remember Cheryl, the casting director, saying, "She, an actress, was so needy, she just wouldn't get out of the room, and she was really good, but . . ." She lost the job because she was so needy, and it was just a reading. She kept asking questions, like, "Is that all right?" and the director was present, too. Even though as an actor I'm hoping to get in on the movie, I really felt I was presenting myself differently as a result of class. I kept reminding myself, "I'm not a victim, and I'm equal with these guys." By Friday they asked if I wanted to read for a part, and I read for a part, and they gave me a little part in the movie.

Wayne: I had a reading on Monday for a contract role on a soap opera, which I've done before for Marty Cohen, who's in New York and comes out here about once a year and looks for talent. I've never gotten a response, so I went in saying, "I'm going to get a second meeting." That was my goal. And I went in and, you know, he started to look at the résumé, and I pulled him out of it: "I just got engaged." And we started talking about that for a little bit, and, you know, we had a little bit of an experience, and then I read. And then I jumped up. "You know what? Gotta go. Thank you!" Just like, I'm not needy, I just did my thing and then I left. And they called me back about three hours later, put me on tape on Tuesday, and during the taping session—you know, it's a whole deal, they put a microphone on and the whole thing—I did it, and I did it again. And I would never have done this before last week, but I really knew I could nail it, and I didn't on that take, and I looked him right in the eye and said, "I really can nail this; just let me have one more shot." It was just like me talking to a colleague or something. He said, "Okay, great, go for it." And I did it, and he came over and said, "Thank you." I mean, a really heartfelt thank-you, as if he were talking to a colleague, like I said. I never have had that experience before. I don't know if anything will come of it; I think it's promising to see the shift in my perception and how it affects my work and the business. Prior to the work we did last week in class, I would never have asked for a second reading. I would have, you know, sort of said, "Ah, I blew my chance," sort of given away my power, which I think I've done by being a victim. And I even coached myself when I felt myself kind of getting manipulative. I was being super polite, saying, "Yes, sir," and "No, sir." I spotted it and said to myself, "Come on, what are you saying?" and I dropped it and just talked with him like an equal. So I look forward to getting it in my body.

Tracy: I just had a commercial audition, and you know how I can be overly polite and really quiet. So I decided to be very present and to riff on whatever anybody said. I came in, and you could tell they were a little loopy from all day of seeing people, and so anytime they said something, I sort of said something funny about it. It just built and built. It was like that spirit of "Yes! And . . ." that we studied before, and it just got funnier and funnier and funnier, and we were making each other crack up. And I messed up a couple of times, but I was very goofy and very loose with it, and got another callback on it.

4

Heightening the Experience

Rules and Tools

Consider the rules and tools that we have been exploring to create better interviews:

Victim

- Don't be a victim.
- Be the host.
- Interview the interviewer.
- Don't want anything.
- Create an experience.
- Keep the interviewer from looking at your résumé.
- Avoid discussing your credits.

- Avoid laughing at anything that's not funny.
- Avoid unnecessary apologies.
- Avoid making the other one up (giving the upper hand).
- Avoid making yourself one down (taking the lower hand).
- Avoid being on best behavior.
- Avoid complaining or talking about your problems.
- Avoid badmouthing anyone.
- If conversation lulls, tell another truth.
- Avoid reacting to interviewer's negativity.
- Remember it is a conversation or a meeting, NOT an interview.
- End it when it has ended.

Authenticity

- Start with a truth.
- Don't pre-plan the truth line; it should be in the moment.
- Avoid unnecessary questions.
- Be authentic—no lying up or down.
- Avoid talking about the interviewer's personal appearance.
- Avoid compliments and flattery.
- Don't manipulate.
- Don't flirt.
- Don't sell yourself.
- Don't con anyone.

Create an Experience

- Be present.
- Don't react to negativity.
- Avoid isolation.
- Avoid the word *I*.
- Avoid telling any stories about yourself.
- Reflection Listening is available if valuable to you.
- Yes! And . . . is available if valuable to you.

When you arrive at the interview it is very important that, you are "present." It is impossible for the interview to go well if your attention is fragmented. Following is a tool for "getting present."

40-Breath Process

Setup

Take forty breaths, pausing briefly between each set of ten. Keep your eyes open. The breaths should be big, not slowly done, but not rushed, in and out through the mouth, drawn to the chest, with an emphasis on the inhale and a relaxed exhale. Right after the last breath, look around the room and identify objects or clothes, by naming them with their color: "There is a blue clock." "She is wearing a green sweater." "That is a black chair." When naming the colors/objects, you must focus on them and commit to the exercise. Don't rush through it.

Follow-Up Question

How do you feel?

Summary

This exercise will put you in the present. The breaths will oxygenate your blood, bringing a charge to your body that you will feel as a tingling in your limbs. If at the end of the forty breaths you don't feel any tingling, do ten more, and ten more if necessary. The tingling is your body's telling you that you have oxygenated your blood, which in turn creates a charge in your body and makes you present. Naming the objects/colors focuses you in the here-and-now in an authentic fashion because you are naming truths about what you see at the present moment. When you feel you are not "present" in the here-and-now and are "split off" or "fragmented" and your victim or manipulation styles are taking over, do this exercise.

What does it mean to be fragmented? According to psychologists Jack Lee Rosenberg and Beverly Kitaen-Morse, "The simplest, most basic type of fragmentation is when something happens in the present that takes you back in time to a similar emotional injury or theme from your childhood. This apparent reenactment of a past injury can make you feel as if you are catapulted back to the time in your childhood when the original injury occurred. The childlike emotions that emerge can feel overwhelming. Then you not only have the current injury to deal with, but you must also contend with the emotional weight and intensity of the childhood injury."[1] When something fragments you in the waiting room (e.g., a disrespectful secretary or a smart-ass actor), try to recognize what has happened. You will notice a shift from a sense of well-being to an uncomfortable one that will affect your interview or audition. You will notice you have become nervous, lost confidence, or feel depressed. After recognizing this shift in feeling, "get present" by doing forty breaths, which you may want to do in the hallway or in a restroom. Then name the colors of objects. This will make you present for a short period of time, and it may be long enough to help you get the job done. At the very least, it will break the spell of the fragmentation.

In order to acquire the next tool for creating and heightening an experience, you should practice an acting focus. Ideally this should be done as an improvisation with a partner, but you will benefit if you only read through the focus and visualize what you would be doing.

Extend, Intensify, and Enlarge[2]

Setup

With a partner, each select a character, then together select an activity and location for an improv.

Rules and Acting Focus

While improvising a character doing an activity and making contact with the location's space set pieces, you should explore extending, intensifying, and enlarging different aspects of your performance. In order for you to respond to your fellow actor, and to move in whatever direction the improv leads you, you must be attentive and *open to going with whatever is happening*. In Part One your acting focus is to extend, intensify, and enlarge any of your *sounds, movements, and postures*. In Part Two you will amplify this to include *feelings, emotions, attitudes, and ideas*.

Part One: Sounds, Movements, Postures

While you are improvising you will discover yourself making gestures, such as a finger scratching a cheek. Enlarge this. The finger scratching now enlarges to five fingers climbing up the face and then enlarges to pulling at your hair. Finally this enlarges into pulling with both hands at your clothes. Make it really big and go with it wherever it leads. Stay in character.

While you are improvising you will discover yourself making sounds: laughing, coughing, grunting, or even whistling. Select one of them and enlarge, extend, or intensify it. And then continue going with it as it becomes something different from how it started, e.g., a cough becomes a howl. Make it really big and go with it wherever it leads you. Stay in character.

While you are improvising you will discover yourself in a particular posture, e.g., hunched over. Extend *that* posture, and then continue extending it into a realm of extra-theatricality. Make it really big and go with it wherever it leads you, e.g., hunched over becomes a character rolling across the stage like a bowling ball. Stay in character.

After about five minutes, go into Part Two.

Part Two: Feelings, Emotions, Attitudes, Ideas

Now that you are improvising and have a heightened self-awareness of what your body is doing, recognize when you have an impulse and go with it by intensifying it. When you have a feeling, intensify and enlarge it, e.g., pleasure intensifies to hilarity; nervous intensifies to terror. Stay alert to the emergence of an attitude. Extend that attitude throughout the body and intensify it. Stay alert to what you are feeling and be available to extending, intensifying, or enlarging it. Go with it! Notice any interesting comments you or your partner make in your dialogue and choose to extend that idea further. Explore that idea. Intensify it.

After about five minutes, end the improvisation.

Follow-Up Questions

Were you on your acting focus?

Did you extend, intensify, and enlarge?

Were you open to going with it or were you guarded and closed? Examples of being guarded and closed would be not responding to your impulses or those from your partner or negating opportunities to go somewhere new, regardless of the reason.

Did you make discoveries and go with them?

Did you inhibit yourself from going with them? Did you interfere with your partner's going with them?

Did you allow the acting focus to lead you through the improvisation or were you more concerned with the improv's evolving story?

Can you describe the difference between feeling open and closed?

Summary

When you are not open to going with what is happening, your mind dictates what you will or will not do. Your mind decides how things should be, and anything that doesn't subscribe to that agenda is declined. This robs you of your true potential and keeps you earthbound when you have the capacity of enjoying real flight.

It takes courage and a willingness to let go of what you think or have decided should happen. Most student actors take direction and simply execute it; a professional actor takes direction and goes somewhere new with it. Direction becomes a mere jumping-off point for the professional.

Once you were open and went with what was happening, did you notice how easily you escalated your initial feelings into full-blown emotions? A slight feeling of frustration might have been intensified to anger and then further to absolute fury by *intensifying* it. An emerging attitude of confidence could have been escalated to one of strength, and then further to one of absolute bravery. You discovered a willingness to intensify what is already happening.

In the last chapter, you worked on losing your victim stance and becoming authentic. The interviews in the last chapter were honest, pleasant, free of manipulation, and became the foundation for having an experience. In the next round of interviews, we will focus on creating, building, and heightening that experience.

General Interview Exercise #4

Setup

Here again, as in all the exercises in this chapter, it is better if you can work with a friend. You will gain knowledge if you read through the exercise, but the experience will be heightened if you actively participate with a partner. One of you will play the role of the interviewer—in this case an agent—and interview the other. Then you will reverse roles. In pursuit of new representation, you, the actor, have arranged a meeting with an agent. The agent should have the actor's picture and résumé on the desk. The actor playing the agent conducts the interview according to his or her own experiences of being interviewed in similar situations. The interview begins when the agent calls out the actor's name and the actor walks into the agent's space. When the agent feels that the conversation has ended, the agent may thank the actor for coming in and end the interview. The exercise ends with the actor's exit.

Use the Tools

When you are being interviewed, practice the tools with which we have been working and also adopt the attitude that you don't want anything from the interviewer. It follows that if you don't want anything, you shouldn't have to sell anything. When your meeting starts, as soon as you say hello, tell a truth about what you see or hear in the office, in the present. If it feels like the conversation is rolling along, you can use Reflection Listening and Yes! And . . .. When the initial conversation that flows from your first truth line starts to fade, tell another truth. Regardless of what goes on in the interview, *never look to see how you are doing*, i.e., don't judge how the interview is going. This may take the form of thinking that the interviewer is not with you or that you are fearful the interviewer doesn't seem to be as into the interview as you are. When you are acting, you do not look to see how well you are performing—you don't want to know the reviews while you're in the midst of an opening-night performance. When you look to see how you are doing you become a victim and put the other person above you. Avoid any form of communication, verbal or non-verbal, in which you are seeking to find out how the interview is going.

After the conversation gets rolling, choose to employ the acting focus Extend, Intensify, and Enlarge, which you worked on in this chapter. You know how to use this acting focus within an improvisation; now be brave and try it in an interview.

When you feel you have made your impact, end the conversation when it is ended.

Workshop Actors' Interviews

In the workshop interviews I coached the actors to extend, intensify and enlarge. Whenever I coached, "Extend that gesture," it was preceded by the actor's having made a natural hand gesture or head or body movement.

General Interview Exercise #4 — Shannon

Shannon: Hi, I'm Shannon.

Agent: Hi. Nice to meet you.

Shannon: You have a turquoise sweater on.

Agent: Is this turquoise? I guess it's a cross between aqua and turquoise.

Shannon: Yes. Like an aqua-turquoise. One is water and one is stone.

(**Book:** *Extend that idea!*)

Shannon: One is wet and moist, and the other is, like, textured.

(**Book:** *Extend that gesture!*)

Shannon: Smooth. Smooth like stone, like jade.

Agent: Yes. It gets smooth when it's in the water, especially.

Shannon: It's like flowing and floating on the water. It is similar to air. Floating in an ocean. It has, like, no control. The stone is sleek and smooth with rough edges . . . with bumps. Like ice.

Agent: Interesting. I feel like I have just seen an entire performance-art piece.

Shannon: You are wearing a silver pin.

Agent: Yes. Actually, this probably doesn't go that well. I got this at an antique store, and it was really cheap.

Shannon: It goes with the black stripes.

(**Book:** *Explore that idea!*)

Shannon: You know the black stripes. It is like a different shade of black. The gray is like black, and it goes with the aqua and it all blends together well.

Agent: And you are wearing lots of purple and lavender.

Shannon: Yes! And the purple heightens my thoughts.

Agent: The purple heightens your thoughts?

Shannon: Absolutely.

Agent: Really?

Shannon: Yes. Lavenders. They say it opens the seventh chakra.

Agent: Let me tell you my favorite color and tell me what it means. I love that deep, deep red . . . like beets.

Shannon: I think they say that is the stomach chakra.

Agent: Does that mean something?

Shannon: I am not completely familiar. There is something about being grounded.

(**Book:** *Extend that!*)

Shannon: You are grounded and connected to the earth.

Agent: If you are connected to that color, does that mean you are grounded, or you are attracted to being grounded?

Shannon: You are attracted to being grounded.

Agent: You may not actually be grounded?

Shannon: Exactly. You are drawn to it. That is what you were feeling at that moment. With purples, it is creativity and being open to the universe.

(Book: *Extend that idea!*)

Shannon: Exploring all the different levels and dimensions of the mind, the mysteries that are surrounding us every day.

Agent: Wow. I feel like I just spent the afternoon at the Bodhi Tree [a spiritual bookstore in West Hollywood]. Have you been there?

Shannon: I have always wanted to go there, but I don't do it because I always think, "Who are these people?" I really want to be there, but I step back into that judgment thing.

Agent: It's the incense getting into your brain.

Shannon: The incense? Oh. There are some incenses that open up your whole sinuses and everything. Did you know that?

Agent: Actually, they all make me kind of dizzy.

Shannon: Dizzy?

Agent: Yes. They are always really too strong for me. I am not a strong incense person.

Shannon: Oh, incense.

Agent: You know, there seems to be no such thing as subtle incenses. It always seems to be overpowering.

Shannon: How about lavenders and citrus?

Agent: A little of it, I guess. Somehow I have a sensitive nose.

(Book: *End it when it is ended!*)

Shannon: Well, there is smell. There is color. There are elements. These are so many things that could change our day. Well, it was a pleasure meeting you.

Agent: Likewise. Thanks for coming in. (*Shannon exits.*)

Book: Interviewer, did you have an experience?

Agent: Yes.

General Interview Exercise #4 — Josh

Josh: Hi.

Agent: Hi.

Josh: How are you?

Agent: I'm fine.

Josh: You have a little box all fastened with rubber bands.

Agent: Oh yes. Let's see what is in it.

Josh: Wow.

Agent: Chalk.

Josh: White chalk.

Agent: Yes.

(**Book:** *Extend that idea!*)

Josh: Let's stick the rubber band right back over it and wrap it back up. Fasten it.

(**Book:** *Enlarge that gesture!*)

Josh: Fasten it right down. We could just get some duct tape and wrap it right down on the table. We could get some nails—

(**Book:** *Extend that!*)

Josh: Some nails and pound them in around it. We could set up trip wires and if anyone got close to it, flares go off—

Agent: All for chalk?

Josh: Chalk is really hard to find sometimes. "I need a piece of chalk. Where can I get some?" You have some sitting right there. You know? Get illumination flares, and that way, you can see who is going after your chalk. You never know who takes your stuff.

Agent: No. It is one of those things.

Josh: You realize, "Oh, man, it's missing." You never think that someone actually took it.

(**Book:** *Enlarge that attitude!*)

Josh: What is going on—

(**Book:** *Enlarge it!*)

Josh: Sometimes you don't—

(**Book:** *Enlarge it more!*)

Josh: You don't really know what is going on. You don't really know if somebody is going to take your car after you park it. Or if you go into an office, you look someone in the eye and say, "Hey. What's up?" That guy could be watching you to see where you put down your coat, because as soon as you put your coat down, he is going to take it. I'm sure you have seen that before: When people just look at you like, normally, and you don't think anything about it, but they are the ones you have to watch out for. They might lift your coat, your shoes.

Agent: Your socks.

Josh: Yes! And socks always get lost.

Agent: You know, like when you go to the laundry room.

Josh: I know. I know. I pulled a sock on the other day. It ripped because I left it in the dryer too long. That is my point.

(**Book:** *Extend that gesture!*)

Josh: I think dryers actually dry them to a point—we have people walking on the moon, we have people spending thirty days in space. John Glenn is going up there and eating out of plastic bags, but what happens to a sock in the dryer?

(**Book:** *Explore it. Go with it!*)

Josh: What happens to a sock in the dryer? Necessity is the mother of invention, but screwing around is actually the mother of invention sometimes. Do you know what I mean? I left the dryer on too long. It was supposed to be fifteen minutes; I left it on for, like, sixty minutes. I came in and the sock was just brittle.

Agent: I see.

Josh: Yes! And you are not wearing socks.

Agent: No. I am not wearing socks.

Josh: I am wearing socks.

(**Book:** *Extend that gesture!*)

Josh: Wool socks.

(**Book:** *Extend it!*)

Josh: (*Stands and pulls pants leg up*) I'm going to pull that way up to the top. All the way up to the top. Have you ever seen that—wear little socks, but they pull them right up to their knees? Everybody had someone in school like that. Right? Had to pull them up to the knee.

Agent: With the stripes at the top.

Josh: Those are the same guys who always wore gym shorts really tight. Me, I put them in the middle.

Agent: You don't pull them up?

Josh: I just let them do what they want. Sometimes I don't touch anything. Sometimes I don't button things up. Sometimes I don't comb my hair. Well, it has been nice meeting you.

Agent: It was nice meeting you. (*Josh exits.*)

Book: Did you have an experience?

Agent: Yes. It was like I was at a stand-up show. I was laughing the whole time.

General Interview Exercise #4 — Lisa

Lisa: Hi. How are you?

Agent: Hi. Good.

Lisa: Good. You have an unvarnished table.

Agent: Yes. Rough.

Lisa: It reminds me of guys with the big tool belts with thirty tools on them . . .

(Book: *Enlarge that gesture!*)

Lisa: . . . walking around and fixing things.

Agent: That is what I wanted this desk to remind me of: big guys with tools belts.

Lisa: Really. It looks like they carved something in here. (*Bending over the table and examining it*)

Agent: Yes.

Lisa: It is like a mini bowling alley.

(Book: *Extend that gesture!*)

Lisa: Have you ever seen one of those stores . . . you go in for a back rub?

Agent: Is that legal?

Lisa: It's like—Is it legal?

Agent: Yes.

Lisa: It is called The Great American Back Rub.

Agent: Oh.

Lisa: There is a whole chain of them all over the United States of America.

Agent: Really?

Lisa: Extending through every state. They are going all over.

Agent: The Great American Back Rub?

Lisa: Yes.

Agent: I have never seen one.

Lisa: They are like human pet stores. You go and you look in the window and there is someone there having their back done.

Agent: Can you tap on the glass?

Lisa: Yes. It might disturb them, though.

Agent: Right.

Lisa: You can do that with the puppies.

Agent: Do not tap on the glass . . .

Lisa: Do not.

Agent: . . . especially when you are looking at the puppies.

Lisa: Right. Your eyes are so blue because of that shirt.

Agent: Oh, yes, I planned that.

Lisa: You planned that?

Agent: No. I didn't plan that.

Lisa: You didn't?

Agent: No. I just like blue shirts.

Lisa: You like blue shirts?

Agent: And blue contact lenses.

Lisa: Are those fake?

Agent: Yes. Just a little bit.

Lisa: So, when you put them in do you get eye-paranoid? I get eye-paranoid. (*Touching her eyelid*)

(Book: *Extend that gesture!*)

Lisa: It is like a mini skullcap that you are supposed to attach to your eyeball. You can imagine it like a toilet plunger. What if it gets sucked on, and it can't come off? That is my image anytime I see someone with contact lenses.

Agent: Who is coming at you with contact lenses?

Lisa: My eye doctor. He comes over and, like, rips the bottom of my eye open because I close it and won't let him come near me. He doesn't like me at all. He rips open my eye and puts in the drugs, or whatever he is putting in, so the eye will expand so you can look in and see the end of the universe in my eyeball.

(Book: *Extend that idea!*)

Lisa: I do believe that these guys are not really eye doctors. They are some sick, mad scientists who have a reverse telescope and can actually see little reflected edges or mirrors, sort of like those mosaic lamps like they put on the posts outside in New York in the Village and stuff. They put them up to your eyeballs. That is how they know about the galaxies, and like, Saturn, and the rings around Saturn and stuff. What they are is—who is that big athlete that runs laps around one of those planets out there, and you see it reflected in your eye?

Agent: Oh. So, what are telescopes then?

Lisa: They are like reading glasses; they are just really long. What is that guy's name? They made two movies about him.

Agent: Steve Prefontaine?

Lisa: Yes. That is exactly who I am talking about. It was Prefontaine running laps around one of the planets out there and the dust . . . (*Shaking fingers*)

(Book: *Extend that gesture!*)

Lisa: He was running so fast.

(**Book:** *Extend it!*)

Lisa: He kicks up all this dust and that is what makes the ether and the ether is actually dissipating, and that is why you don't see it, because he ran so incredibly fast that what happened was the little particles of stuff that were flying off the back of his shoes got so much momentum because he just kept running around, that they are all flying into each other. So, eventually, they are all going to slow down to this incredibly slow rate, like one particle deceleration per billion years, or something like that.

Agent: Then what is going to happen?

Lisa: Well, eventually the rings are going to disappear. Then no one will be able to tell Saturn from any of the other planets, except Mars, because it is all red. You know what I mean?

Agent: Wow. Will we be around for that?

Lisa: If I ever finish my Tai Chi.

Agent: Oh.

Lisa: Speaking of Tai Chi, I have to go to yoga. It was very nice to meet you.

Agent: Yes. Thanks, Lisa. Lisa. See you later. (*Lisa exits.*)

Book: Did you have an experience?

Agent: Yes. Most definitely.

General Interview Exercise #4 — Anthony

Anthony: Hi. How are you?

Agent: Good. How are you?

Anthony: Good. You have a blue box with rubber bands wrapped around it.

Agent: Yes. I do have a blue box with rubber bands wrapped around it.

Anthony: They look like they are being extremely carefully kept.

Agent: Yes.

(**Book:** *Extend that idea!*)

Anthony: Is it like a secret ring box?

Agent: Very secret.

Anthony: A secret decoder ring.

(**Book:** *Explore that idea!*)

Anthony: With all the madness that goes on every day, you could decode it and make it all simple, and that would relax you. (*Pause*) You have a hole in your table.

Agent: Yes. I have a few holes in this table. Natural holes. There is another one.

Anthony: Looks like you cut off a door.

Agent: Yes, it does. Some little door. What do they call them? Dutch doors?

Anthony: A cut-off Dutch door. It is the bottom half.

Agent: Have you been to Holland?

Anthony: No, I have not. (*Taps the table*)

(**Book:** *Enlarge that gesture!*)

Anthony: I have been to Alaska. Glacier-trekking.

Agent: Okay.

Anthony: They do not have Dutch doors in Alaska. They just have a lot of snow and a lot of ice and glaciers. Very cold. Don't ever go to the bathroom at night on a glacier because there are big crevices—

(**Book:** *Go with it!*)

Anthony: It's like being caught in a freezer if you fall into one of those. You need to always stay within the perimeter. Not to mention the fact that when you go out with bare feet because you really have to go to the bathroom, your feet get very cold.

Agent: Why do you have to have bare feet when you go to the bathroom?

Anthony: Because you can't take the time to put on your boots and your socks. You are naked, and you have to get out of your sleeping bag, and it is really cold out. It is like thirty degrees in the summertime on the glacier. Got to run out and do what you have to do. You have to go far enough away from the tent so it doesn't leak back underneath and then come back in and get all warm again.

Agent: Yes.

Anthony: Yes! And don't drink a lot before you go to bed when you are sleeping in a sleeping bag on a glacier. That is just something that you should keep in mind. There is a chalkboard directly behind you.

Agent: Yes, there is.

Anthony: With all sorts of writing on it.

(Book: *Go with that!*)

Agent: Yes.

Anthony: Scribbling and scribbling . . . someone up there all day writing and writing; "I have to get this down on the chalkboard."

(Book: *Intensify that gesture!*)

Anthony: "I must express my thought on the chalkboard. I love the chalkboard."

Agent: Would you like to go to the chalkboard and get rid of some of your aggressions?

Anthony: Yes. (*Writing on board*)

(Book: *Enlarge that sound!*)

Anthony: I feel much better now.

Agent: I'm glad.

Anthony: I put a nice tip on that stick of chalk for you.

Agent: You did.

Anthony: Thank you for giving me the largest piece of chalk in the chalk case.

Agent: You look like a big-piece-of-chalk kind of guy.

Anthony: I am a big man with a hearty appetite, and I like a big piece of chalk. Big! That is what I like. This office is big. I like that! That is a big rubber band. I like that, too.

Agent: I like my big rubber band.

Anthony: That is sweet. You could wrap that around your chalk box a couple of times.

Agent: Thank you.

Anthony: Now, no one can get at the chalk. "You want some of this chalk? You talk to me."

Agent: It looks real secure.

Anthony: It is. You are right. When the chalk creeps come in, they look at that and go, "No way. I am not touching that. Where is the easy-access chalk? That is what I want. Where is the easy chalk?"

Agent: Right.

Anthony: (*Gesturing around the studio*) "I don't want the stereos. I don't want the garbage can. I don't want the two ladders. I want the chalk." That is what they say. Yet you foil them each and every time.

Agent: I try.

Anthony: Rest easy, chalk. You are not going anywhere. No one is taking you, chalk. You are in the chalk box. Thanks for letting me use the chalk.

Agent: You are welcome.

Anthony: Sure. Thanks for seeing me. It's been fun.

Agent: For me, too. (*Anthony exits.*)

Book: Did you have an experience with him?

Agent: Yes. I had an experience with him.

Follow-Up Questions

What happened when the actors were on focus and responded to the coaching? An experience happened when they enlarged, extended, and intensified or explored. Frequently, it took the interview to a whole different level.

Did you notice any victim behaviors?

Did you see any manipulation?

Do you think the interviewers were kept from looking at the résumés?

When you were being interviewed, were you able to enlarge, extend, and intensify on your own?

How was it to choose to end the interview when you thought it was time to do so, instead of waiting for the interviewer to determine the ending?

Did you ever look to see how you were doing?

Summary

Using this acting focus in an interview should create physical spontaneity, the same spontaneity that you exhibit and feel when you're playing a sport. Fully playing a sport requires complete participation "in the moment," and the result is spontaneity.

Spontaneity is always authentic. It is impossible, physiologically, for spontaneity to be inauthentic and it never has room to embrace a victim stance, hidden agendas, or manipulation of any kind. In addition, the boldness required and displayed by you when doing this acting focus is the physiological opposite of producing a victim stance. Victims are neither bold nor brave. *Everyone employing this acting focus will eradicate any semblance of being a victim.* When people are spontaneous, they present themselves as being very attractive—think of actors performing, dancers dancing, athletes playing; they are always attractive, always. Your spontaneity always gives the interviewer insight into the real you, not into an inauthentic performance that you presented in your first interview. This attractiveness will be further highlighted by the contrast between you and other actors who will appear unattractive because of their inauthenticity and victim stances. Your spontaneity will be a breath of fresh air.

When you enlarge, extend, intensify, or explore, you *turn a dry, fearful interview into an exciting showcase* in which you shine from your authentic essence. Your essence or core self is who you were before you got fettered with the junk of your dysfunctional families and the junk of dealing with the power structures and sleaziness of show business. That unfettered personality is your core self. You seldom get to act from this core because of life, because you have to deal with the cop yelling at you and your husband behaving inappropriately and your agent not returning your calls and the casting director changing the sides on you the minute you walk in the door after you have spent four hours preparing them. All those situations are catalysts that pull you out of your core self. When these negative situations occur, you behave according to the way you have been conditioned to behave, i.e., in a way that you think will get you what you think you want. You come from your defense system, which is neither authentic nor your core self. However, there is one time that allows you to reveal your core self. The one time your authentic and unfettered core self is always right there is when you are playing a physical game, e.g., tag, volleyball, soccer. Playing is the one time you act from and reveal, spontaneously and authentically, your core self.

The acting focus of enlarge, extend, or intensify puts you into a state of playing with the moment. How do you play with the moment? As humans we experience sudden inclinations to action without conscious thought. These impulses take the form of gestures (e.g., scratching, gesticulating, shrugging), voice (e.g., coughing, groaning, laughing), ideas, and feelings. These impulses emerge according to the different circumstances in which we find ourselves. This acting focus takes advantage of these impulses and heightens them in an authentic fashion by using the full body. A hand gesture utilizes energy from the wrist to the fingers only. Enlarging or intensifying this gesture activates the whole body in an expression of the original impulse. When you work this way you are giving *a true performance of yourself.* You take a dry question-and-answer interview session and turn it into a revelatory presentation of yourself in a heightened fashion. You get your picture put into the "hot" file because the interviewer had a good time and looks forward to seeing you again. He or she got a sense that you are a performer with tremendous potential for acting a role. Whatever you enlarged, extended, or explored became the springboard to travel to new places with the interviewer in the form of an experience. This heightened energy is infectious. You will be remembered and get called back.

How do you know what you should intensify, enlarge, extend, or explore? Any moment of the meeting is available. If you do any gesture, it is available for enlarging or extending. If you make a sound, it can be enlarged. If an emotion gets triggered, you can intensify it. If any subject comes up, you can coach yourself, "extend or explore that idea." Whatever you do, follow it up by going with it! If you get off your acting focus, you can always jump back on by playing Yes! And . . . after the very next comment from the interviewer.

What Do You Have To Lose?

What you have been doing at interviews probably hasn't been bringing you the results you want; therefore, you have two choices: You can continue doing what you have been doing or you can change your behavior to see if this new behavior brings you better results. Do you remember the definition of insanity? Continuing with the same behavior and expecting different results. You now have a different behavior available to you. You can try it to see if your batting average improves, or you can keep doing what you have always done and continue getting the same results.

In the last interview you had the opportunity to observe whether or not you felt the actors were too big or too imposing. This raises the question, "Is it possible to go too far with this acting focus?" The answer is both yes and no. It's always possible to go too far, but if you go into an interview thinking there's a danger of going too far, you will undercut yourself, not reap the benefits, and carry with you the victim's fear. It will also stifle the fun that could be happening between you and the interviewer.

Should you actually go too far, the interviewer will stop you. "Stop. Stop. Calm down a second. So I want to look at your résumé here. Who are you? What have you been doing?" The interviewer will do only that. He or she will not put up with a crazy person in the same way that he or she is not going to put up with a victim. But it is very unlikely that you will go too far. Fear of that simply provides you with a reason for not trying your new focuses. If you create an experience and make an impression, you will stand out and, if you do go too far, the interviewer will only think, "This person is nuts," which is a great deal more desirable and attractive than, "Damn, I have to take care of this wimp." Some great actors are nuts and you are not going to be dismissed because you are edgy. Even if the interviewer thinks, "This person is a total wacko," it is to your advantage. You might just be able to bring that wackiness to a role. It is not to your disadvantage for a casting director to think you are a wacko because you will be noticed and your energy will be appreciated. You will probably be brought back to see if you can transform or pour your unique energy and edginess into a character.

Casting directors love to discover new, terrific actors. Tony Chagrin, an agent at Metropolitan Talent, tells this story about the first client he signed: "She had great training, but not a whole lot of credits. When she came to meet me, she was really punked out, wearing big club shoes at eleven in the morning. I was twenty-five; I didn't care. The other agents saw her tape and agreed to meet with her. I told her to dress down, and she came in there wearing combat boots and a black slip. I thought it would be awful, but everybody liked her. She had a great meeting. It opened my eyes early in my career that you can do things differently and succeed, even in a room with a bunch of stuffy agents at eleven in the morning. She had very few credits, but we signed her off her training and how nutty she was in the room, and it worked." He added, "It's not about trying to impress them. It should be about presenting yourself as a commodity in an industry."[3]

It is low energy, your victim stance, and your manipulating the situation that cause you to fail. If you created an experience at your interview, but left thinking, "He must think I'm a little nuts the way I carried on about the stratosphere and black holes and the peas in China," do not be concerned. More often than not you are going to stand out. They are going to love you because they can sit back, have a good time, and be entertained. You have turned an interview into a successful audition. Everyone else may have turned his or her interview into a funeral.

You may feel a little pushed to come up with something, but even that feeling is preferable to those of being a victim that you experienced before you started this work. Even if you felt rather safe and sane in your earlier interviews, you should now understand that it is better to feel a little bit on the edge and have an exciting interview. You have to keep this in mind as you think about being too big. It is working on that edge that allows you to reach deep inside yourself to find a greater source of energy than you usually have at an interview.

This is the moment of artistic crisis. When human beings are in crisis, they physiologically and unhesitatingly reach inside themselves to find sources of greater energy. If you are walking across a street, you are using only a tiny bit of energy. If then you perceive that there is a speeding car moving toward you, in that tenth of a second your body provides you with a massive increase of energy to get you out of the way. The body responds to crisis by releasing energy. If your new focus made you feel as if you were walking a tightrope, that might be wonderful because your body was creating that much more energy. This energy increases your presence in the interview and allows you to have an experience. You cannot have an experience with someone else if you are not bringing energy to it. Being out on the edge creates energy and allows you to be uniquely spontaneous, or spontaneous in your own unique way. *ER* casting director John Levey says, "All you have is your own uniqueness. If you try to homogenize yourself, you're diluting your uniqueness. If you try to guess what they want and become that, you're strategizing and you're not in the moment. All you can do is what you can do. And that's not a limitation. Your responsibility is to become as interesting a person as you can."[4]

Fear

Being on the edge as you face the crisis of what to do next may initially provoke fear in you. A good deal of that fear comes from your behavior as a victim. This is exacerbated by the nature of your profession: You face rejection numerous times a week from interviewers, potential employers, business connections, and ultimately, from audiences. These issues of rejection contribute to the victim inside of you, and some of the manifestations of that are nervousness and fear. More accurately, the victim stance is an attitude, and the fear and nervousness are emotions. Dealing with that fear and finding the courage to do what you have to do despite the fear begins with honesty.

As novelist Neil Gordon writes, "Did you ever, when you were a child, stand on a cliff above a lake and will yourself to jump? You know there is no danger. That when you find the will to step into the air, your body will writhe to its balance, that the water will crash around your face in a brilliant flash of green, and that, laughing, you'll rise to the surface in a tunnel of bubbles exploding against the sun. Yet with all you know, with all you want to jump, before the act itself a paralysis overtakes you.

"It is not the height, it is not the cold of the water—these are there, but are not what stop you. It's the consciousness that before you is a decision, and, trivial or not, once taken, it cannot be revoked."[5] Once you start to extend, intensify, or enlarge, there is no going back. You are making a commitment to creating an experience and you have no idea how it is going to play out. You are taking a trip into the unknown. Go for it. Go on a journey with an unknown destination, but know that wherever it leads, you and the interviewer will have an authentic and exciting experience in the "now."

End It When It Is Ended

How do you know when to end an interview? When you have a feeling that suggests it is the time to end it. Feel when it is ended, and choose to end it. The meeting continues as long as you feel comfortable and are a part of an experience with the interviewer. Sometimes the cue will be the interviewer dropping his or her head to look at your résumé. An effective and authentic ending line is, "It is nice to meet you." Even though the meeting is ending, that line keeps you in the present tense, as opposed to, "It was nice to meet you." "It is nice to meet you" is also totally free of any victim stance, as opposed to, "Thank you for seeing me" or "Thank you for your time." Thanking the person is a manifestation of your victim stance. I know it's polite, but you have to stop being on your best behavior if it puts the interviewer "one up to you." "It is nice to meet you" makes you equals. When you choose to end the interview, don't race out of the room. That is inauthentic. You are being gracious in words and attitude, but your body is sending the message, "I can't wait to get out of here!" If you find that you frequently don't know when to end the interview, write about that issue in a journal or diary. Question whether or not you may be afraid of disappointing the interviewer. Are you taking care of the interviewer? Caretakers hate disappointing anyone. Also, people being taken care of usually dislike the caretaker. This is because they know that the caretaker wants something in return and is dishonest for not saying so. They feel manipulated.

Can you end the interview too quickly? Certainly, but not likely. And if you do, the interviewer will probably say, "Where are you going? Sit down." You can then choose to sit down. If your goal is to be remembered and to be seen again, it is better to leave the interviewer wanting more of you. If you have been doing the exercises, you have gone from being a victim and acting in a manipulative manner to having an authentic interview in which you provide an experience for the interviewer and yourself. Your picture and résumé will be put into an active file, not the trash.

Isolation

If you are hoping to change your interview technique by reading this book without doing the exercises, you may end up giving a performance, which may result in your not being spontaneous regardless of who the interviewer is. In fact, you may ignore the interviewer and perform in isolation. When you practice Extend, Intensify, and Enlarge you experientially learn how to play with the moment that is occurring *between* you and the interviewer. This results in an experience between you and the interviewer, not a performance that could make you look desperate.

A Successful Experience

Mark: From watching it, the bottom line of what it gave me is this is the first interview level where, if I were the interviewer, I would want to see this person again. I think that the energy that everyone had was like you want to have this person back in your office again to have an experience with them.

Andrew: I always had this preconceived notion of wanting to let the person see who I am, but I realize now, I wasn't doing it. I was putting on an act. I was *telling* them who I am. Now I see this is how you do it. And they really see who you are, because you are *showing* them who you are. It's just like that acting rule—show, don't tell.

Christina: Before the interview you don't have to think of things you want to get in. And, you can be nutty; you don't have to worry about that.

Brian: People were so interesting to watch.

James: What I noticed, even more from being the interviewer, was that their energy just clued you in. I found myself getting in sync with her, which if you were sitting on that side of the desk all day, wouldn't you want? That was cool.

Tracy: It created a lot of presence for everyone; more energy. Also, for me it really felt more relaxed because I was able to use tools that I already learned. I felt by using those tools it made it easier for me and I usually find interviews very difficult.

Lisa: When I first think about employing a tool at an interview like this, what comes up for me is, "Is that going to be authentic?" But it seems that after I employ it, the other approach that I was using was inauthentic.

Wayne: When you commit to be on focus—I mean just go for it and not look back and I was watching people do it—as soon as someone was committing to be on focus, this energy came and the interview was great and totally successful.

Josh: Sometimes the interviewer looked stunned at the beginning; well, let's put the "stunned" into context. The context is they are used to dealing with actor after actor with the same old bullshit that they have to take care of: They have to host you, take care of you, create the topics of conversation, be responsible for the meeting, ward off your inauthenticity and manipulation. All of a sudden a breath of fresh air and spontaneity comes in the door, they just might be stunned but it is a good stunned. You are not walking in and pissing on their desk.

Liz: I felt like I was at a party. When I spoke, I didn't know what was going to come out of my mouth next. Watching the others, it also looked like everyone was at a party because they were having so much fun. Everyone was just so interesting!

Anthony: Doing this interview reminded me of past interviews that have been successful. It had that same feeling to it, but in the past I always thought of it as luck or we happen to get on that subject of, "Boy did we click on that," and I thought it was out of my control. I realize now that much of the time in old interviews I conducted myself from a defensive habit, ready to back up at the slightest sign of something is wrong, instead of going and playing, exploring and intensifying.

Krista: I discovered that I didn't have to hit upon the one subject that I know about. I'm serious. The real excitement was when the subject came up that I didn't know beans about. Because I was exploring and enlarging through things like gesture, I rose to the occasion and there was enough stuff there to feed whatever the subject was for as long as that subject needed to be on the table. I felt that when I extended my gestures, my voice and my being followed and I got all excited about the green sweater the interviewer was wearing and I'm into the fabric business all of a sudden! When I said, "House of Fabrics was sold yesterday for 150 million dollars!" I didn't know I was going to go there. I didn't even know I knew that fact. I think I read the newspaper yesterday. This all came from the inside of just following the body. It was very exciting, just like a hot improv; it was all from physicalizing, physicalizing, physicalizing. What my body did, the rest of my being followed along because the rest of my being is enveloped by my body.

Laura: It felt very liberating to be able to extend the acting exercises we use in our Improvisation Technique to the casting office. Sometimes I used Reflection Listening and I found it very effective in keeping a connection.

Linda: For me it was very liberating to not want anything. I didn't pursue an agenda. I really just went in there to enjoy the person. And watching it, it seemed true for everyone: There was not anything anybody wanted. It was just two people that had an appointment talking.

Dorian: About, "Don't look to see how you are doing": I didn't see anyone at all do that, and I certainly didn't do it either. It never occurred to me to check in and see how I was doing. I was so caught up in the experience to bother seeing how I was doing.

Louisa: I felt like I was not worried about checking in. I was not worried about trying to give a good impression or trying to be on my best behavior. It allowed me just to go.

Veronica: I also felt very free that I was going in there to improvise, that is it. I don't have to think about, "What am I going to say?" I am going in there to see what is there.

Sean: That big neon sign of agent just disappeared.

Shannon: I felt a connection to the person I was talking to. In my past, it has been rare. Even if it was a good interview, I didn't feel that there was anything going on. I realize now that what I used to do was to turn the casting director into an object instead of a person. Working this new way they become a person, and it's so much more fun to be with a real person instead of an object. And it must feel better for them. I know I hate it when someone treats me like an object.

Larry: This is a favorite story that actually happened: A friend of mine was auditioning for a commercial twenty-five years or so ago, for Mountain Dew soft drink. These were black-and-white commercials, and they had a hillbilly theme: "Mount Stompin' Good." He goes in there . . . twelve people behind a long table: clients, writers, directors. Everybody's there. So he sits down, and he's a portly man, and they talk for a minute. They ask him to take off his shoe and sock so they can see his bare foot because they're going to have to shoot his bare feet. He says, "Okay." He takes off the shoe. He takes off the sock. He reaches down, still seated, pulls his foot up, and tries to put it on the end of the table, and when he does, he lets out an atomic fart. It is the biggest thing he has ever heard. The room is stunned. He doesn't know what to do. He's turning beet red. He doesn't know anything to do except leave. He gets up and leaves. Then he realizes he's forgotten his shoe and sock. He has to go back and grab that and leave. He's just humiliated. He thinks his career is over. It is awful. He gets home to his house and his agent calls. He's gotten the job! He said, "What?" Then he realized, having seen 400 people that day, all they could talk about at the end of the day was the guy who farted. (*Laughter*) He created an experience. Now, I'm not recommending that to anyone, but it was a legitimate experience. That's what they remembered.

Your Progress

After your first interview in Chapter 1, you may have felt that you would never be able to clean up the dishonesty and victimization from your act. You may have even experienced fear. However, after absorbing a few new tools and rules you must feel that you have made progress in transforming your interview techniques. Continue to practice on your own and you will make further progress.

Assignment

You can practice what you have learned in non-business conversations, i.e., at parties or in any social situation. Don't tell anybody what you're doing; just practice it on your own for five minutes. Don't evaluate yourself while you're playing because you will kill your spontaneity as you look to see how you are doing. Follow your rules, get on focus for five minutes, and then say to yourself, "Cut." You can then think about and evaluate what you have done. How you do the self-evaluation is important. Start by considering the reactions of the people with whom you have been practicing. If they seemed to be engaged and to have a good time with you, that's the only evaluation you need. If they stopped listening, or pulled away, or started bullshitting you, then it wasn't working. If you come to that conclusion, you will want to look at why. The underlying issue will always be, "Were you really doing it?" You may think you were doing it, but instead of totally focusing on enlarging or extending and intensifying, what you were really doing was watching the other person's reaction, which distances you from your authentic focus because you had another agenda—you were asking yourself, "Is this working?"

Honesty and authenticity are frightening and threatening because most of the time they confront you head-on with your negative traits; therefore, you're going to come up with dozens of reasons not to practice your new techniques.

When, and only when, you get feedback that a casting director or an agent thought you were a crazy person should you be concerned about being over the top. Until then, don't be afraid of being too big or your interview behavior will remain cautious and your batting average will not improve. You now have a challenge and the tools to meet it. If you don't rise to the challenge, then your interviews will continue as they always have. Be brave—try something new.

5
Tracking and Changing Behavior

J osh: I had a great interview, and as I walked out, they said, "We'll see you." And I said, "I hope so." Then I immediately realized that was a victim expression and thought to myself, "Oh God, what an idiot."

Tracking Behavior

Since you began this work on your interview technique you have become more aware of your victim stance and inauthenticity. In order to change a behavior, you must have a heightened awareness of that behavior or else you will continue with it without being aware of it. When you keep track of something, it is called tracking. Tracking includes observing the occurrence of a phenomenon, when it begins, how long it lasts, and what ends it. Tracking is a very important tool in changing behavior because it increases your self-awareness of something—in this case, a behavior that you want to change.

If we want to track and change our victim behaviors, we need to review the manifestations of victim behavior. What are the things that we do that are read by others as signs of our being victims?

Victim Stance Manifestations

- Having negative physical posture.
- Being nervous.
- Being needy.
- Not speaking loud enough to be heard.
- Not respecting what you say.
- Not listening to others.
- Making unwarranted apologies.
- Laughing at your own unfunny jokes.
- Laughing at the interviewer's unfunny jokes.
- Putting yourself down.
- Complaining.
- Acting overeager.
- Acting overly appreciative.
- Using false flattery.
- Asking permission.
- Seeking approval, brownnosing.
- Making the other party one up, or giving away the upper hand.
- Looking to see how you are doing.
- Asking unnecessary questions.
- Badmouthing someone unnecessarily.
- Giggling or laughing nervously.
- Making excuses and not taking responsibility.
- Being defensive.
- Not being who you are.

Other Manifestations That Take the Form of Manipulation

- Lying in any form.
- Running a con, such as being overly enthusiastic or being a flirt.
- Being self-absorbed.
- Fantasizing to avoid responsibility.

Do you recognize any of these behaviors as yours? The more you clean up victim-stance manifestations in your life, the more you will clean them up in your interviews and in your careers. To change a behavior usually requires a great deal of work and/or much discipline. People go to psychiatrists for years to change their behaviors. The next tool we will learn has great power for changing behavior. It doesn't take a great deal of time, costs nothing, and is able to be performed alone. It presents you with a wonderful opportunity but will require a little bit of discipline.

Keeping Your Score[1]

The tool that you can use to help yourself is called Score. Here is how you use Score: Identify one, two, or three victim manifestations as those that you have. During designated time periods, observe yourself, and during these periods if you catch yourself doing any of the identified behaviors, make a mark on a scorecard. That is all you have to do—it is as simple as that. *Just keep score.*

After Josh came out of his interview and noticed that he had used a victim's exit line, "I hope so," he would—if he were keeping score on being needy or giving away the upper hand—have taken out a paper or an index card and made a check mark on it. That is the whole tool. You have an opportunity to clear out all your victim behaviors with a technique that simple.

Scorecard

Let's talk about the scorecard itself. The best scorecard is two scorecards. One is fixed in your house. Hang up a chalkboard or a dry-erase board or a mirror. The size of these scorecards makes the process more effective. The second scorecard is portable: a pad that you carry with you, an index card, or an automatic clicker that keeps a constant tally. These would, of course, be used in conjunction with the permanent board at home. You would transfer your marks from your portable scorecard to your permanent board. You could also place something in your pocket, such as a leaf or a chewing-gum wrapper, to keep score. At the end of the day if you have five gum wrappers in your pocket, you must add five marks to your permanent scoreboard. Use your own variations on any of these. When you observe yourself exhibiting one of your designated behaviors, just make a mark. That's all. Monday you have twelve marks; Tuesday, ten marks; Wednesday, eight marks, . . .

Designated Time Periods

Control the time period when you keep score. I suggest you choose a specific time period to be observant. Choose a reasonable time frame, something realistic that will allow you to have a shot at doing this, then commit to it. You are wrong if you think that you can start doing it on a twenty-four-hour basis. You can't. You will fail and give up. Instead, walk into the water slowly. Designate a specific time period. "Tomorrow I am going to keep score between noon and one P.M. Tonight I will do it between seven and seven-thirty." Start with a half-hour, an hour, or even just ten minutes. Start with something that is reasonable. It really doesn't even take any extra time on your part because you are doing it while you live the rest of your life. Then once you have two or three days of success, increase the time. Go to two hours. Keep increasing the time until it docs become a twenty-four-hour time period.

What To Score?

The choice of which behaviors to score is up to you. From the list of victim stance manifestations, do you recognize any that are yours? Choose one, two, or three of your victim manifestations. Then say, "Okay, I am going to keep score every time I do one of these behaviors." Examples of these behaviors might be laughing at something unfunny, apologizing unnecessarily, and telling lies. These are examples of what you can score. One to three manifestations to score should be sufficient, but if you become aware of another manifestation, keep that score also. Adding to your scoring-eligible victim manifestations means you are becoming more self-aware. But first start by selecting your most serious issues.

Theory

Do not try to improve your score or beat yesterday's score (fewer ticks). Improving has nothing to do with this. You don't have to do anything but keep score—that's all. If you try to beat your score, you will screw up and become an even bigger victim. Don't try to achieve anything. Keeping score is the whole tool. Avoid adding improvements to the tool.

When you keep score, you are making a commitment to changing your behavior. You are becoming open to receiving help and inspiration—you are becoming open to receiving extra energy. Making this commitment requires self-awareness, which will lead to the end of your judging your unwanted behaviors as you learn simply to observe them. Observing without judgment is a necessary step before changing any behavior.

At the beginning of this chapter, Josh told us what happened to him after leaving a successful interview. When he walked out of that interview and said, "I hope so," the next thing he said to himself was "Oh God, what an idiot." That was putting himself down for what he saw as victim behavior. The more you judge yourself and put yourself down about things you don't want to do anymore, the more you commit to repeating them. If he were playing Score, instead of saying, "I'm such an idiot" at that moment of self-observation, he would just make a little score.

Making the score replaces the self-judgment. The feeling accompanying that will be so much more gratifying than the feeling that accompanies calling yourself an idiot. Scoring it creates a positive feeling because you made an active commitment to something constructive. To be proactive in the pursuit of success feels better than giving in to self-loathing. Every time you put yourself down—"I'm such an idiot"—you become the person you are putting down. You become what you resist. When you keep score, you are not resisting the self-limiting behavior, you are observing it. You are not saying it is good or bad. You are simply observing it. *Score is a pause to let you know what you just did.*

Results

Over time, and not a very long time, you will stop engaging in these behaviors if you keep score. When you have to stop for a few seconds to make that score mark and then transfer it to your big scoreboard, you are committing to the process of self-observation or self-awareness. The more self-aware you become, the more responsibility you take for your behavior. And it will begin to happen spontaneously. You will get tired of taking the score for a particular behavior. You understand that you could stop taking the score if you stop that behavior. When you understand, you just stop engaging in the behavior, without effort or discipline. It should happen automatically as if you are in the groove in an improv. After taking score for a while, you will take responsibility for stopping the behaviors that you have been scoring. This is the power of authentic self-awareness.

It requires a commitment on your part to keep score, but do not fool yourself that keeping mental score will do the trick. Those scores disappear. This weakens the process, which loses its impact.

It is very important that you don't try to beat your score each day. Just keep score! Then take what you get, whatever your score is. *Don't judge it.* Just make your marks and take whatever you get—even if your score increases over a week. There is no desired scoring outcome. It is all about the process. *If you play this for any significant amount of time, the unwanted behavior will disappear.*

Your victim stance behaviors are unconscious behaviors. You don't know that you are laughing nervously at something that is not funny. You just do it automatically. You don't know that every time you speak you preface the sentence with the words, "I'm sorry." This is unconscious behavior. No one is consciously a victim. When you play Score, you bring your unconscious behavior into consciousness. When you are fully conscious of your behavior, you have the power to change—and you do.

Keeping score is foolproof because you don't have to try to change your behavior. All you have to do is commit to keeping score. As you increase the increments of time, do not be concerned that your scorekeeping periods are not career-related. Victim stance behavior can show up in your social and family life. Remember, not being authentic and lying keep you oppressed. The more you perpetrate these behaviors, the more you commit to being oppressed. The irony is that you are your own oppressor.

Journal

While playing Score, you may have revelations about yourself, and if you want to go deeper into them, write about them in a journal. You may write about anything that comes out of this process. Make sure that when you write you don't put yourself down. Think of your journal as in-depth scorekeeping. When you finish your journal entry, start another paragraph with this question, "Where is the lie in what I just wrote?" Then read over what you wrote and look for the answer to that question. Then write about any lies you found.

Getting Started

Dorian: I have to look for a day job tomorrow and I have an interview with an agent. Should I put off playing Score until the next day?

Book: You can start Score tomorrow. Score is something you can do parallel to other things in your life. It is usually necessary to play Score while just doing your normal life, which, in your case, includes looking for a day job and meeting with an agent.

Dorian: I really want to sign with this agent. How can I change my behavior by tomorrow?

Book: Forget changing your behavior. You have learned exercises and tools for how to handle an interview. Just do that. In addition, if you care to eliminate the victim from your life, not your professional career, your life, you can play Score. Obviously, if you eliminate it from your life, that will include eliminating it from your professional career, too. All you need to do is make a little tick mark every time you do something that you have predetermined that you would like to stop doing. You now have a tool, which presents you with an opportunity for changing your behavior—why not use it?

Mark: How important is it to have the big scoreboard at home?

Book: Very important, and to be in a place where you see it. Every day you walk by it, and there it is. Using the larger scoreboard is a bigger investment in yourself, and the gravy is, it quickens the process.

Laura: How long should we keep score?

Book: Don't self-sabotage the power of the tool by doing it for one hour a day for two days and then quitting: "It didn't work for me." Anything that is a behavior change takes a bit of time. Start with short periods of time and gradually increase your time periods until you are doing it around the clock. If you have been really doing it, by the time you get to full days, your behavior will gradually disappear.

Wayne: What is the best scorekeeping method?

Book: Tick marks. One, two, three, four, and then a line through it for the fifth one.

The only problem with Score is that there is a strong likelihood that you will choose not to use it. You want a cheap, easy tool and here it is, but you have to make a commitment to it. While playing Score, you are going to become more aware of your behavior. The more you become aware of it, the quicker you will stop engaging in that behavior. This is a quick process that could be the beginning of changing your life.

What do you call a victim who is proud of it? A martyr.

Attitudes

You must know people who manifest their personalities through attitudes—through the belief that no one loves them or that they are superior to everyone else. Or maybe they have sunny dispositions, or they are very wise, or they are very macho, or they flirt with every person of the opposite sex. Personalities that call attention to themselves have an attitude at their center.

There is a character-creating acting focus in Improvisation Technique based on the creation of a character from-attitude that could be very helpful in preparing for an interview, specifically in the area of transforming your victim stance into one of authenticity. To begin with, let's learn how to do the acting focus for character improvisations, then we will learn how to apply it to the interview work.

Assignment

Make a list of five attitudes, worded as succinctly as possible. Examples: I'm sweet; I'm lonely; I'm angry; I'm the best; Nobody loves me; I love life; I'm pretty; I'm the smartest; Screw you; I'm very happy; I'll try anything; I'm impatient; My way! Use one of these examples or create your own *attitude line* by stating the attitude as a personal expression. An attitude line is effectively articulated when your body easily and immediately responds to it. Articulate it in three words or fewer. In each attitude there should be only one idea expressed, so avoid *because*. Any attitude with the word *because* will automatically contain at least two ideas about the meaning.

Avoid attitude lines that are so cerebral or intellectual that you have to take time to think about their meaning before your body responds. You've got to word them in such a way that your body has an easy, immediate, visceral, and *total* physical response. A line isn't intellectual just because it includes an intelligent word. There is nothing wrong with "I'm conservative" if your body responds to it. Your body might respond to *conservative* just as immediately and easily as it would to an emotional word, such as *happy*. An ineffective attitude line would probably be "I tend to be conservative." It has too many words, too many beats, too many issues, and it waters down what's important. Get to the point and you will find that "I'm conservative" or "I'm a conservative" is much better.

If you have an attitude line that you like, but suspect that it is ineffectively articulated, you can rewrite it. Let's take "I don't want to get involved" as an example. What's wrong with "I don't want to get involved"? Too long. Too wordy. Two beats or ideas instead of one. (First beat: "I don't want." Second beat: "to get involved.") Also, it is built around a negative, "I don't," instead of any variation of "I am." There are some attitude lines that are effective and are built around negatives, but in general, their being negative is a warning sign that they should be rewritten. Look at the opposite way of saying the same thing. What's the opposite way of saying "I don't want to get involved?" What's another way of saying "I don't want to get involved?" without negative words? You could try "Stay away," or "I'm aloof," or "I'm detached," or "I like safety."

Always personalize the attitude line. Don't just write the key word, e.g., *angry*. Make it "I'm angry."

Be careful of lines that use the pronoun *you* as the subject, e.g., "You don't love me." This line is about someone else. Rewrite it so that it's about your character, e.g., "I'm unloved." On the other hand, lines that start with *nobody* or *everybody* frequently work well, as in, "Nobody loves me" or "Everybody understands me."

Any time your line includes the words *I am*, contract them to *I'm*. The shorter the line, the more singular the feeling and the more impact it will have, and your body response will be more effective. The best attitude line has only two or three words; more than five and it needs rewriting.

The attitude line should not be ambiguous. There is nothing ambiguous about "I'm happy." But how about "I need to be happy"? No good. You've got the issue of *need* and the issue of *happy*. So, rewrite it. Instead of describing what you need to feel, describe what you *do* feel. If you need to be happy, you are what? Sad, depressed, angry, scared? You decide. Put an *I'm* in front of your choice and you have an effective attitude line. You could even go with "I'm unhappy," if you can say the line and allow your whole body to have a physical response. If not, something is wrong with the line.

Demonstration of an Attitude-Line Test

I'll give you an example of how to test an attitude line. Let's take the line "I need to be happy." Repeat the line to yourself, "I need to be happy, I need to be happy." Don't improve the line. Let your whole body respond immediately and totally to that attitude. Do you notice how hard it is? Do you feel that? It's vague. Now let's try it with "I'm sad." Repeat the line to yourself, "I'm sad, I'm sad." Let your whole body be immediately and totally affected. Can you respond to it? Notice how specific it is. That's all we're talking about. Even though you clearly understand and know what "I need to be happy" means, it just does not create an immediate and totally physicalized body response. "I need to be happy" first creates a feeling of sadness around the phrase "I need" and then a feeling of happiness around "happy." These signals cancel each other out, creating a feeling of vagueness. A good attitude line has got to be a singular feeling without ambiguity.

You can do this test on any attitude line. After you have selected the line and reduced it to the fewest words, do the test. See if you have a complete body response to it in one second. You will know immediately if the line is a good one. If you feel wishy-washy and can't get a hold of the line, it failed the test. Rewrite or change the line.

When rewriting an attitude line, ask yourself, "What do I really mean?" or "What do I mean by that?" Say that your first draft of a line is, "You can't always get what you want." You're suspicious of the line's efficacy because of the number of words, because *can't* is negative, and because the subject of the line is *you*." Ask yourself, "What did you mean by, 'You can't always get what you want?'" Your answer might be, "The reality of what has taken place has not met my expectations." Then ask yourself, "What does that mean?" "I'm disappointed." Now you have an effective attitude line that means what you originally intended. If it doesn't mean what you originally intended, go back to your original line. Keep asking questions about its meaning to bring it down to the one thought, the one feeling, the one expression.

After the list is complete, do an attitude-line test for each attitude line to determine which one impacts you sufficiently to *select it as the attitude line you will work with in the improvisation*.

Attitude Lines[2]

Once again you do not have to participate in this improv to benefit from its lessons, but you will learn more quickly if you work with a partner.

Setup

Sit on chairs next to each other.

Rules

You are going to do a warm-up before the improvisation. During the warm-up, you will be led to your acting focus. Later you will learn the character, activity, and location choices for a series of six improvisations, and you will then go immediately into the first of these by moving your chairs around to approximate the first location. This moving process should take no longer than ten seconds. After you improvise the first scene for about five to six minutes, immediately rearrange your chairs and go right into the second improvisation. You will continue doing your series of improvs for half an hour. There is to be no discussion about the rearrangement of the location. You go into it immediately, then go with it.

Warm-Up Exercise

Put your feet flat on the floor. Take forty breaths, pausing briefly between each set of ten. Keep your eyes open. The breaths should be deep, not slowly done, but not rushed either, in and out through the mouth, drawn to the chest, with an emphasis on the inhale and a relaxed exhale. Right after the last breath, look around the room, and identify objects by naming them with their color: "There is a blue clock; she is wearing a green sweater; that is a black chair." When naming the colors/objects, you must focus and commit to it. Don't just throw the naming away. Similar to truth sentences, these are complete sentences and not fragments.

After breathing and naming the objects and colors, stop and briefly make eye contact with your partner. Now sit and breathe normally, calmly, gently. Sit up straight, look straight ahead, and observe your own breathing. Now, *silently repeat your selected attitude line to yourself over and over to the exclusion of all other thought*. Without urgency, repeat it. Keep your eyes open. Allow the line to tell you its line reading. Keep repeating it silently throughout the exercise. The line will always tell you how it wants to be said.

Read through the following directions and then go slowly through them. If an extra person is available, he or she can coach the directions. Send your attitude line as a message to your *feet*. Move your feet in response to your attitude line. Let your feet respond to the attitude. Keep your eyes open. Move your feet around until you find the position that best reflects that attitude. Let your feet be the feet of someone who has this attitude. Physically explore to express that attitude line with your feet. Your toes, arches, heels, and ankles are expressing that attitude. Don't let go of that. Keep repeating the line to yourself silently.

Now add your *legs*. Allow your legs to be totally impacted by your attitude. Move them around until you find the expression in your legs. Each part of your leg should be adopting that attitude. Let your knees reflect that attitude. Don't let go of your feet. Now attach your feet to your legs. Don't let go of your feet and legs.

Go up to your *midsection*: stomach, abdomen, pelvis, and genitalia. Send the attitude as a message to the midsection of your body. Move that part of your body around until it is an expression of that attitude. Allow the midsection of your body to be totally affected by the attitude, and when you find it, adopt it, hold onto it, and don't let go. Attach it to your legs and feet and don't let go. Check to make sure you haven't let go of your feet and legs. The whole lower half of your body is now an expression of that attitude. You feel that attitude with every part of your lower body. Don't let go of it. You can keep moving your body parts around, but don't let go of the attitude. Keep repeating the line to yourself with meaning. Avoid urgency.

Now, let's add your *chest*. Move your chest around until your chest is an expression of that attitude. Let your chest reveal the attitude. Move your chest around until it receives the message of the attitude and reflects it. Show us the chest of someone who has that attitude. Don't let go of that.

Now, go to your *shoulders*. Send the attitude as a message to each shoulder so that each shoulder is an expression of that attitude. Feel the attitude sitting on each shoulder. Move each shoulder around within that attitude. Express the attitude with each shoulder. Don't let go.

Now go down to your *elbows*. Express the attitude with each elbow. Move your elbows around within the attitude until you find the expression of the attitude with your elbows.

Now your *hands*: *wrists* and *fingers*. Each hand is affected by the attitude. Each hand is an expression of the attitude. These are the hands of someone who has this attitude. Move your fingers around until they best position themselves in that attitude. If there were a spotlight on your hands alone, we could tell what your attitude was by looking at your hands. Don't let go. Keep repeating the line to yourself with meaning.

Feel the attitude moving up and down your *spine*. Feel it sitting on each vertebra point. Move your spine around until it is a complete expression of that attitude. How would a person who has that attitude sit? That is what your spine should be showing us. Feel your spine shaping to the attitude. Don't let go.

Now, your *neck*. Let your neck be totally impacted by your attitude. Don't let go of any parts of your body that you have already visited.

Now, go up to the top of your *head*. Feel the attitude sitting on the top of your head. Keep your eyes open. The attitude is sitting on the top of your head. How much does it weigh? Don't intellectualize it, just feel it. Whatever that attitude weighs, that is what it feels like on the top of your head. Allow it to sit there and allow your head to react. Move your head around until it captures the attitude. Don't let go of your body and what we have done so far.

Now, come over the top of your head and let your *eyebrows* reflect this attitude. Express the attitude with your eyebrows. There is no right or wrong way. It is just what you feel. Move your eyebrows around until you feel the right setting for you. Then hold them in place and don't let go.

Now, go down to the tip of your *nose*. How does your nose feel when you have this attitude sitting at the tip of your nose? Let your nose express the attitude. Don't let go.

Now, your lower *lip*. Feel your lower lip manifesting this attitude. Move your *lower lip* around until you have it. Add your *tongue*. Let your *whole mouth* express the attitude. *Smile* with this attitude. *Frown. Scowl. Breathe* with this attitude. Allow your attitude to affect your breathing.

Now, *increase the volume of your inner line-readings and send it as a message to all parts of the body at the same time.* Allow your body to respond. When you find the position that best reflects this attitude, hold onto it. Focus on not letting go of this physical expression of your attitude. Keep it in your body and don't let go. Retain this and say your line out loud. *Actors, one at a time, say your lines out loud.* Now, tell each other your lines. You may overlap. Don't let go of your bodily attitudes. Continue to tell each other. Now, get up and *start walking*. Keep expressing the attitude with your body. Walk with this attitude. Keep telling each other your lines. Your focus is to hold the attitude in your body and on your face. Walk to the farthest point away from each other and say your lines louder. Use your whole body to say your lines even louder. Louder and bigger!

Now stop speaking! Don't move. Don't let go. *Hold that attitude on your face and in your body! Feel the expression on your face. Feel the way your muscles are holding themselves in place. This is what you must not let go of throughout the entire range of scenes.*

In a moment, you will start your first improv scene. You will quickly set up your chairs and go right into the scene. Throughout the improv, *your acting focus is not to let go of this attitude in your body or face.*

There is also a rule—*you may never again say your attitude line out loud.* You should repeat it to yourself frequently in order to help you retain your body alignment and facial expression, but never out loud.

Feel the way your muscles are working together right now. Your focus is to hold onto that. Feel the expression on your face. It is like a mask. Your focus is to keep it on. Through all of the scenes, you must retain this muscle composition, this facial expression. This is your acting focus; you are not to let go of your attitude. It is a physical acting focus.

Acting Focus

Retaining the attitude on the face and in the body.

Guidelines for the Improvs

- Each improv should last about five to seven minutes.
- Stay on your acting focus of not letting go of your attitude.
- Avoid hanging out.
- Silently repeat your attitude line to yourself.
- Do an activity.
- Use all your improvisational skills as you discover different activities.
- Make contact with the location space set pieces.
- Use and respect your space objects.
- Discover objects to use.

- Repeat your attitude line to yourself frequently, but don't say it out loud.
- Avoid talking about each other's attitudes.
- Don't let your particular attitude keep you from involving yourself with your partner.
- Help your fellow actor solve problems.
- Show us; don't tell us.
- Remember that acting is doing.
- Go still as the improv ends.
- Rearrange your chairs for the next improv's location. The next improv will then begin.

If another person is available you might ask him or her to call out the improv changes and establish when each improv is over.

First Improv

You are five years old and in kindergarten. Stay on your acting focus. Don't let go of your attitude. You may repeat your attitude line to yourself as often as you wish, but you cannot say it out loud. Retain it in your body and face. When the improv ends, go still and silently repeat your attitude line to yourself.

Second Improv

You're now fourteen years old and you're at McDonald's. Arrange your chairs into a new location setting, quickly. Stay on your acting focus. Don't let go of your attitude. Retain it in your body and face. You may repeat your attitude line to yourself as often as you wish, but you cannot say it out loud. You must retain it in your body and on your face. When the improv ends, go still and silently repeat your attitude line to yourself.

Third Improv

You are twenty-one years old and you are setting up a campsite. Stay on your acting focus. Keep expressing your attitude with your body and your face. You may repeat your attitude line to yourself as often as you wish, but you cannot say it out loud. When the improv ends, go still and silently repeat your attitude line to yourself.

Fourth Improv

You are forty years old at an office Christmas party. Stay on your acting focus. Keep expressing your attitude with your body and your face. You may repeat your attitude line to yourself as often as you wish, but you cannot say it out loud. When the improv ends, go still and silently repeat your attitude line to yourself.

Fifth Improv

You are sixty-five years old and at your country club. Stay on your acting focus. Keep expressing your attitude with your body and your face. You may repeat your attitude line to yourself as often as you wish, but you cannot say it out loud. When the improv ends, go still and silently repeat your attitude line to yourself.

Sixth Improv

You are ninety years old and at a senior citizens' home. Stay on your acting focus. Keep the attitude on your face and in your body. Don't let go of the attitude. Say it to yourself as often as you wish. Stay on the acting focus. *After about four minutes*, you are approaching the end of the improv. During the final minute, you are going to find a place to integrate your actual attitude line as a line of dialogue. However, it will be the last thing your character says, for you will immediately die after saying it. You indicate your death by simply lowering your head.

Immediately following the last improv, do the following Character Step Out process for releasing the attitude's effects on your body.

Take forty big breaths, four sets of ten breaths with a tiny pause between each set. The breaths should be big ones, not slowly done, but not rushed. Inhale and exhale through the mouth. The emphasis is on the inhale, which you should take to the center of your chest. Relax your exhales. Keep your eyes open. Then, do full-body stretching in different directions and speak gibberish. Allow this to continue for fifteen to thirty seconds. Now, with your fingertips, gently pat your face. Each tap is an expression of, "Hello. I love you. Hello. How is my old friend? I love you." Then bend over and pat your knees for ten seconds. Finally, make eye contact with each other for a few seconds.

Follow-Up Questions

Were you on your acting focus?

Did you retain the attitude in your face and body throughout the improvs?

Did the attitude affect, change, or realign your body?

Did you discover a character totally influenced by your attitude line?

When you found yourself thinking, did you think as the character or for the character?

Did you feel your character was affected by your attitude through the entire life cycle?

Character Armor

Extreme attitudes can make for a life of freedom or enslavement. In real life, attitudes are formed in early childhood and become conditioned responses to dealing with the world. They form the personality that becomes physically embedded in the person's muscles, which is the reason we walk the way we walk, talk the way we talk, and respond the way we do to stimuli. Some people's attitudes are healthy and expansive; others', self-limiting. We develop our basic attitudes as individual defensive styles as a reaction to the way our parents and the environment treated us in early childhood. As we grow, our bodies align themselves to continue that attitude. That body alignment then becomes a part of the physical being and forms what psychologist Wilhelm Reich calls *character armor*. We all go through life wearing our own character armor. In the real and personal world, the taking on of this attitude and its accompanying armor is not authentic to the child. It is a role the child learns to play. Actors can profit from this by realizing that when they create a theatrical character, they have to take on the attitude and the armor that goes with the role.

When you play a theatrical character, you are putting on another's armor. This can be clunky and inauthentic unless you remove your own armor first. We began this character armor improvisation by taking forty breaths because this is the quickest way to remove your armor. Forty big, explosive breaths oxygenate the blood and put an electrical charge into your body. You may feel dizzy after you take the breaths. If you immediately focus on something you can *see*, whether it is by making eye contact with your partner, or by looking around the room and naming the objects and their colors, the dizziness should go away. Then, focus on your own natural breathing to begin the process of focusing on the character's attitude and realigning your body accordingly.

With this work, you must remember that choosing an attitude alone, without allowing it to affect your body, is worthless. It must affect the body in order for it to become ingrained as the character's armor.

The Scripted Character

The most important thing about character work is living in the character's body and possessing his attitude. When you can do that, you will also spontaneously think and feel as the character does.

While every character has an attitude, it can alter in the way that it altered over the lifespan of your character in the improvisations. You felt and said your attitude line at age fourteen very differently from the way you felt and said it at age ninety, but the attitude line stayed the same. Let's say that your basic attitude line is "Nobody loves me." At age fourteen, "Nobody loves me" means "I feel like killing myself." At age ninety, it might mean, "Nobody loves me and that's the way it is. That's life. What else is new?"

At different story points, your character may be impacted differently, your attitude line may alter, but it will remain the same basic attitude line. If not, you are wrenching or changing the character. A real person's, or character's, basic attitude does not change. Psychotherapy teaches us that it's not about changing who you are, no matter how lousy life is for you, but rather about becoming conscious of your attitude so you can learn how to deal with it, to experience it authentically, to make the most of your situation and not become a victim of it. Then you can move beyond your own limitations. It is never about changing the person who goes through life saying, "Nobody loves me," into an "I'm happy" person. It is false for your character to change attitude lines midstream.

The character's attitude affects everything you as the actor say and do. It impacts how you hold your body, walk, pick up something, think, and relate to other characters. During the improvisation, you should have discovered that your attitude spontaneously influenced every single acting impulse and choice. It colored all your improvisational dialogue and affected when you spoke, what you spoke about, and how you spoke. This will also be true with memorized dialogue. Even though the author has chosen what you say and when you say it, the attitude will totally affect *how* you say the lines.

While the author of a script probably did not employ a specific attitude line in creating his characters, he or she certainly imagined, visualized, and created a specific and different personality for each character. The foundation of that personality is the character's attitude.

Characters don't know their attitude lines. A character's attitude line may be "I'm stupid." That doesn't mean that he thinks he is stupid. It's the actor creating the character who knows the attitude line. If you do have an intuitive, negative response to the attitude line articulation, consider it. For instance, you might substitute "I don't know" for "I'm stupid."

Alternative Set-Ups for Improvs

Age 5: Birthday party	Nursery school playground	Day-care center	Kindergarten, teacher is late	First day of kindergarten
Age 14: McDonald's	Jr. High School, planning school newspaper	Jr. High School, bio lab	Jr. High School, waiting for graduation ceremony	Video store
Age 21: Setting up campsite	Card party	Wedding reception	Miniature golf	Lovers' Lane
Age 40: Office Christmas party	Paris restaurant	Hotel restaurant	Community theater rehearsal	Parents Without Partners meeting
Age 65: Country club	History museum	Art museum	Beijing restaurant	Rome restaurant
Age 90: Senior citizens home	Cruise ship	Church bingo night	Arts and crafts class	Friend's funeral

Now let's apply this acting focus to our interview work.

Attitude Line — "I Am"

Take everything off your lap. Sit up straight with your feet flat on the floor. Take five big breaths—not slowly done, but not rushed—with your eyes open. Inhale and exhale through the mouth. The emphasis is on the inhale, which you should take to the center of your chest. Relax your exhales. Take five more deep breaths. Look around the room and name objects and colors, e.g., "The floor is gray. There is a silver lamp. There is a green wall." Don't just say "gray, silver, green." Make a short truth sentence with the objects and colors.

You are going to do an attitude line preparation. You can do this by reading the exercise as you do it. Or, for better effect, have someone else read it out loud and you respond. Begin by observing your own natural breathing. Now silently repeat to yourself the following attitude line: *"I am."* Repeat it to yourself over and over to the exclusion of all other thought. Allow the line to tell you its line reading. Keep your eyes open. Without urgency, keep repeating it throughout the exercise. The line is only two words—"I am." Keep repeating the line to yourself and send the line as a message to your *feet*. Move your feet around until your feet take on your attitude line, until your feet are expressing that attitude line. When you feel your feet are expressing it, add your *legs* without losing your feet.

Allow about ten seconds for each body-part coaching. As you go through your body parts, actually move that body part until you feel it has been affected by the attitude and is taking on the attitude. When you find it, hold it and don't let go.

Now go up to the *midsection, genitalia, waist, and lower stomach*. Move your mid-section around until you feel it affected by the attitude line.

Now go to the *chest*. Keep repeating the line to yourself. Move your chest around until you feel it affected by the attitude line—until your chest is expressing that attitude. Go to your *shoulders*. Do one shoulder at a time. You want that attitude sitting on each shoulder, *elbows, wrists and fingers*. Don't let go of the body parts that you have already visited.

Move your **spine** around until you feel that attitude sitting on each vertebra. Go up to the *neck, top of your head, eyebrows, tip of your nose, lower lip*.

Add your *tongue* and your *breathing*. Let your *whole mouth* and your breathing express the attitude. Breathe with this attitude. Allow your attitude to affect your breathing. Increase the volume of your inner line-readings and send it as a message to your whole body. Stand up and walk around the room and continue to have a complete body response to your attitude line. Allow about two to three minutes for this section. Return to your seat and stay on focus.

Follow-Up Questions

Stay on focus while you answer the following questions.

How do you feel right now?

Do you feel empowered? Strong? Calm? Confident? Aware? Proud? Assured?

Do you feel good? Of course you do—those are very comforting feelings to have. What you are feeling right now is not to be a victim.

Summary

If you coach yourself with the attitude line "I am" in the waiting room before an interview, or if you coach yourself as you walk into the office, you will not be a victim when the interview begins. There should be nothing phony about you—you will be totally authentic.

If anybody were to ask you in a social situation who you are, this is your answer—"I am." Your answer is not, "I am an actor," which is saying what you do. Your answer is not anything you might say, i.e., it is not verbal. The answer is a body experience. Your "I am" attitude line allows you to have an authentic experience of who you are as an individual. This is who you are. This is how you felt when you were born, before you developed your defense system. William James, psychologist and philosopher (the first professor of psychology in an American university, 1875), said, "The greatest discovery of my generation is that a human being can alter his life by altering his attitudes of mind."

General Interview Exercise #5

Setup

For our next general interview exercise, the acting focus is going to be the same as in General Interview Exercise #4—Extend, Intensify, and Enlarge. It is also suggested that you choose to come into this interview with your "I am" physicalization in place. Once you are in the interview, you should practice extending, intensifying, and enlarging. In addition, you are going to employ and practice all the tools that you have learned. The interviewer is not going to be identified in order to communicate that this is an approach for all interviews.

———

Read through the following transcripts and then take the opportunity to practice the exercise with a partner, each playing the interviewer and the actor.

Workshop Actors' Interviews

General Interview Exercise #5 — Shannon

Shannon: Hi there.

Interviewer: Hi.

Shannon: I'm Shannon.

Interviewer: Hi. It is nice to meet you.

Shannon: You have a big kitchen set up here.

Interviewer: Yes.

Shannon: A Martha Stewart kind of kitchen.

Interviewer: Yes.

Shannon: You could whip up a big party.

Interviewer: It has everything.

Shannon: You have a big range. Good for catering parties and things like that.

Interviewer: Yes.

Shannon: You have a microwave. There are theories about the microwave, that they are causing the El Niño effect in the weather. (*Shaking arms and hands*) I think it is a trumped-up thing by the Weather Bureau of the United States. Actually, microwaves are . . . actually, they are doing research on microwaves. They shoot microwaves into the atmosphere, just changing the entire weather pattern of the entire world. They are doing it. They are causing all these crazy problems so that it is all controlled. It is not El Niño. It is produced by the United States Defense System. That is crazy. There is a whole conspiracy going on about microwaves. Did you know that?

Interviewer: No.

Shannon: Yes! And there is also that thing about Diana's death, that it was an assassination, and that the driver was hit by these microwaves when he was driving, and that is what got them in an accident because it threw him off. That is what they can do. They can actually do this now. There is a big conspiracy that is going on. It is just amazing. Don't believe anything that you read in the news. It is all monitored.

Interviewer: Monitored?

Shannon: All monitored completely. Isn't that amazing?

Interviewer: What you read or what you see?

Shannon: When you are reading, you can't really read because all these great powers are controlling what is out there, and the truth is out there, but you have to go find it. It is out there, and it is accessible, but you have to go find it. So don't believe what you read, like in *Time* magazine or *Newsweek*, or what you see on TV news, especially cable, because they are all controlled by money and the House of Windsor. It all goes back to the House of Windsor. That is the problem. Look into it. But keep it quiet. (*Places her finger to her lips and does an exaggerated eyewink*) It is all the House of Windsor. That is a huge white wall.

Interviewer: It is.

Shannon: It reminds me of a canvas.

Interviewer: Yes.

Shannon: You could probably use it as a canvas. You could just throw paint on it. Maybe you could finger-paint. Did you ever finger-paint? Just go up and get it all painted up, and just go for it, and what ever happens, happens? You never know what you will create. Sometimes I go to a museum and think, "I could do that," and you know what, you could do that. You could do that. You could probably become the next Vincent Van Gogh or something. Truly.

Interviewer: I can't.

Shannon: You can. We all could—we just don't know it.

Interviewer: Oh.

Shannon: I mean, he just did it. He didn't go to school for it. He just did it by experimenting and studying. He didn't start painting until right before he died. Did you know that? His brother loved him so much that he supplied him with money. He was like the National Endowment for the Arts. You could have someone be your sponsor, too. Wouldn't that be great?

Interviewer: I could just paint the walls all day?

Shannon: That would be so great. Think about it: You have people come in here, and you take meetings and they will see it because it will be a permanent fixture there. You never know. I mean, you could become another Vincent Van Gogh.

Interviewer: We could cut off little pieces and sell it.

Shannon: Yes! And you could frame them, and hang them up in other parts of the room. It could become a gallery. It would be fantastic. All the space and all the creativity . . . just breathe it in. It makes you feel great.

Interviewer: Sure.

Shannon: You have a black bust sitting on your shelf.

Interviewer: Yes, I do.

Shannon: Wow.

Interviewer: I don't know who put that up there, actually. It was here when I got here.

Shannon: That long neck is beautiful.

Interviewer: It is kind of regal.

Shannon: Yes. Very regal. You never know who was the model for that. Very striking; very regal, though.

Interviewer: It looks like an Indian or Asian or something.

Shannon: Yes! For the Japanese culture, the neck is everything. That is why they wear the kimonos off the shoulder—because it shows the neck off.

Interviewer: Really?

Shannon: It could be Japanese.

Interviewer: It could be.

Shannon: You have a very comfortable-looking corduroy shirt on.

Interviewer: It is actually a jacket, but it is very comfortable.

Shannon: I like that. It makes you look very comfortable.

Interviewer: It is very comfortable.

Shannon: It looks very soft.

Interviewer: It keeps me warm. This place gets cold being so big.

Shannon: I bet. It is nice, though. I have been to casting places that are so tiny that they make you feel small.

Interviewer: Yes. We were lucky. This is just how the space came. We are eventually going to put up walls but, yes, it is very comfortable.

Shannon: The floor looks very comfortable with all the knocks and scratches on the ground. Very comfortable.

Interviewer: Lived-in.

Shannon: Lived-in. Anyway, it's nice to meet you.

Interviewer: Nice to meet you.

Shannon: Bye-bye.

Interviewer: Bye-bye.

General Interview Exercise #5 — Anthony

Anthony: Hi.

Interviewer: Hi.

Anthony: Nice to meet you.

Interviewer: Nice to meet you, too. Have a seat.

Anthony: Thank you. There is a large, brown briefcase on that coffee table over there.

Interviewer: It is. It is actually not mine.

Anthony: What could be inside there?

Interviewer: I don't know.

Anthony: Something mysterious in the weathered brown briefcase. Dare we look?

Interviewer: Uh?

Anthony: No, of course not. That would be awful, to absolutely open up the briefcase and look inside there. You never know what might be in it. It just stays there. That is where it stays. "Nobody touch the briefcase."

Interviewer: Okay.

Anthony: Warning to all the office members.

Interviewer: I was going to touch it.

Anthony: You can touch it, but be forewarned. That is all I'm saying. I have seen a lot of brown briefcases in my day, and that is a dangerous one.

Interviewer: Really?

Anthony: That baby could blow at any minute.

Interviewer: Maybe we should leave?

Anthony: If you hear ticking, then we are out of here. Don't be fooled by the rainbow mug next to it. That is there to fool you. That is why that is there. "Oh, I am so happy, the rainbow mug. Everything is great."

Interviewer: I had no idea I was living in such a world of illusion.

Anthony: Yes! And that silver lamp over there—that is an interrogation lamp. That is what that is. Yes, we will get some answers with that. "What is in the briefcase?" "I'll tell you in a minute." There is a big wooden expanse up there with a lot of framework.

Interviewer: Yes.

Anthony: You could add a second floor up there and use it as a hideout. Your own Anne Frank hideaway. Or, it would make a nice tree house and you could look out over your kingdom—absolute control over who comes to see you and who doesn't. The signal for lunch would be a swinging light. It is a great thing. It all depends on who you are. (*Pause*) Your desk has eight legs.

Interviewer: Yes.

Anthony: Making it the sturdiest desk possible.

Interviewer: As opposed to my chair that keeps sinking.

Anthony: See? That is because it probably doesn't have eight legs.

Interviewer: No. Just one.

Anthony: When they were making this baby they said, "Let's make the sturdiest desk possible. What do we do? What do we do? What do we do? I got it. Eight legs!" (*Bending over*) What is under the desk? It is another brown briefcase, that is what it is. "Everybody run!" Well, it is much too dangerous in here for me. I must bid you adieu.

Interviewer: So soon?

Anthony: Yes. All good things must end . . . or not. Bye.

Interviewer: Bye.

General Interview Exercise #5 — Lisa

Lisa: Hi.

Interviewer: Hello, Lisa

Lisa: This is a big room.

Interviewer: It is bigger than we need, yes.

Lisa: You could do a lot in here, maybe have a party after a nice day, do something crazy. Maybe play a game or something when you are feeling down. I don't know.

Interviewer: I guess so. We could play basketball or something.

Lisa: You could bring people in here just to play basketball under those big fluorescent lights.

Interviewer: Yes, big fluorescent lights.

Lisa: Does it zap your energy in the middle of the day? Do you get drained from the noise from the vibration— *zeeeeeeeeeeeee.*

Interviewer: No, I just think that they are going to fall on me, that's all.

Lisa: That is a good thing, too. You can go, and you are always walking, and you are always moving, and you always have this hesitation sort of stance that will keep you alive with fear and, I don't know, juice, juice from just wanting to be alive without having these fall on you. In the middle of a workday, you could be playing basketball and have these lights not only making this excruciating buzz noise but then the idea that they might fall on you just brings so much excitement into the game, beyond the eliminates of playing and the energy and the blood. Just the energy of playing the game and the lights and the possibility of them falling on you and they slowly, radioactively burn your insides.

Interviewer: Wow.

Lisa: Yes! You have a couch over there.

Interviewer: Yes.

Lisa: You could have a nice afternoon nap after your game, after your near-death experience. Mmmmmmm. This is a small table.

Interviewer: Yes.

Lisa: It has the possibility of being huge.

Interviewer: This table?

Lisa: Yes! Just take some of that plank wood up there and expand the table. You can do a lot of things with this table. You could turn this table over and put these horses on top of it. You could create inventions. Instead of basketball, you could have people come in here and create things with your table and, you know, it would be a whole new art form. "Come into Mark's office and create something out of the table." That will be the idea.

Interviewer: Wow.

Lisa: Wow, indeed. You ever get splinters from that? It seems like that would be one of the downfalls of having an old wooden desk.

Interviewer: It hasn't been a problem.

Lisa: You could get little shards stuck in you from your computer. That is a real common problem. It is actually not the plastic from the buttons; it is the layer of plastic that goes over it that has the plastic imprinted on it. You can get a letter stuck on your fingers. That is the problem. Actually, the real problem is if you can't type and you have an old computer and those letters get rubbed off. If you can't look and see where the letters are, you are in big trouble.

Interviewer: So is handwriting safer? Is that what I should do?

Lisa: No, because of the splinters. You can't win. Don't write anything.

Interviewer: Dictation.

Lisa: Dictation. That is the only way. That is why they do it. That is why they started it. Dictation is a whole other can of social worms because the whole culture that grew up around dictation was based on the man telling the women what to do and she does it. So there are a lot of feminist issues surrounding dictation.

Interviewer: I get myself to do it, so it is no big deal.

Lisa: You dictate to yourself?

Interviewer: Yes.

Lisa: Then you avoid any of the problems.

Interviewer: I have no feminine issues to deal with.

Lisa: That is right. You can get off on the whole misogyny thing. Wait, you don't get off on it. You get off the hook on it—the issue. (*Pointing at holes in desk surface*) You can see the floor through there. It goes all the way through.

Interviewer: Yes. It is minimalist furniture.

Lisa: Yes! And if you were in school and had a desk like that, that could be very convenient. You write the answers on your knee. You stick your knee beneath the hole and you can see the whole thing. And there is no suspicion involved, because all you are doing is moving your knee. But as you wrote further and further down your knee, you would have to move closer and closer to the desk.

Interviewer: You would have to stretch a little.

Lisa: Or you could just put your leg up a little higher. I don't cheat, ever. I have heard about that scenario, but I would never get involved with anything like that. I'm sure you haven't, either.

Interviewer: Never.

Lisa: This place is huge.

Interviewer: Yes.

Lisa: Hellooooooo. Nothing. I've never tried an echo that didn't work. When you do that, nobody knows what you are doing. I just want to assure you that is what it was. I wasn't doing some kind of birdcall.

Interviewer: A valiant attempt. I appreciate it.

Lisa: Well, it is good meeting you.

Interviewer: Well, it has been nice to meet you, Lisa.

Lisa: Take care.

Interviewer: Okay.

General Interview Exercise #5 — Josh

Josh: Hi.

Interviewer: Hi.

Josh: I'm Josh.

Interviewer: Nice to meet you.

Josh: You have a little tea set up behind that cardboard over there.

Interviewer: That is what the cardboard is for.

Josh: You are hiding the Nestea so no one can see it.

Interviewer: So no one can see it.

Josh: Come back in the middle of the night and pull back the cardboard and mix up the Nestea, and you have a little Nestea party all by yourself.

Interviewer: All by myself.

Josh: I would like to join you for a Nestea party sometime.

Interviewer: Thank you. Are you a big Nestea fan? It is actually not mine.

Josh: Your desk has some little holes in it.

Interviewer: It does.

Josh: You could put a little rope through this and a little rope through that end and bring them around, and tie it up, and pull it like a sled like the Indians did when they had those poles. (*Arms and hands make panorama gesture*) When they lived on the Great Plains and had the great migration.

Interviewer: Oh, the American Indians.

Josh: Yes, the American Indians and the great migration with the hundreds of horses pulling the big, long poles with the animal skins stretched out with all of their belongings and all the babies crying. You could just take this here and pull it down Hollywood Boulevard on the back of your car and take the whole office downtown.

Interviewer: Put my kids in the back.

Josh: A small float. It would be a tiny little parade with only one float going down Hollywood Boulevard. And along with your kids there, you could take some of your office stuff there, too. You could put your files on it.

Interviewer: They might fall out.

Josh: Yes! And if they fell out, they would make this little trail of pictures and résumés down Hollywood Boulevard. Then you could head east toward Broadway. How fitting! A trail from Hollywood, across the country, to Times Square, of pictures and résumés! And everyone would know you . . . Johnny Résuméseed.

Interviewer: Then I would have to get rained on.

Josh: Yes! And each picture and résumé would grow into a giant career. (*Sighs and then groans*) It doesn't rain in Hollywood. Have you ever seen any rain in Hollywood for more than five minutes at a time?

Interviewer: No, almost never.

Josh: Yes. And it is hard to drive when the roads are wet. You know, when it gets that slick feeling (*Sliding back and forth in the chair*) it is uncomfortable and you are finding all of that muck and dirt that has been gathering up, you take one step and it is like you are on the worse laboratory floor that you have ever been on; sliding around.

Interviewer: Yes.

Josh: They have the little sign that says, "Danger" in English on one side, and then "Danger" in Spanish on the other side.

Interviewer: What does it say?

Josh: In Spanish, *piso* is "floor."

Interviewer: Especially funny in a laboratory.

Josh: There are marks all over your floor.

Interviewer: Tape marks. For camera marks.

Josh: It seems like one of those mosaics. If you squint your eyes—

Interviewer: Oh, yes.

Josh: If you squint the right way, it is like a picture of Jesus or something. I don't know, a puppy or something. You know those magic-art things that they have? It is like one picture over and over again. You stare at it, and all of a sudden one eye goes lazy, and your eyes start to cross and bug out and you don't see it. Then, all of a sudden, you look at it the right way and you see it. All of a sudden, it is like Jesus is looking at you and you are completely freaked out for the rest of the day, or a puppy or something, and a picture of Marilyn Monroe. Then you're thinking, "What the hell does a puppy have to do with Marilyn Monroe?" It is that hypnotic light thing. That is what it is. You have all these suggestive things in here. Somebody comes in—like the whole pattern on the back of that wall—somebody comes in and they have the opportunity to trip out. And on that note,

I think it is time for me to trip on out of here. It's really nice meeting you.

Interviewer: Very nice. Thank you.

Josh: Bye.

Interviewer: Bye.

Follow-Up Questions

After doing the exercise ask yourself the following questions:

When you played the part of the interviewer, did you have the feeling that you had to take care of the actor?

Did you have the feeling that you were being manipulated or lied to?

Did you have an experience?

When you played the part of the actor, could you have extended, intensified, enlarged, or explored even more?

Did you enter the interview with your "I am" in place? How did it feel?

Did you incorporate your other rules and tools? How did that feel?

Summary

Extend, Intensify, and Enlarge

When you extend, intensify, and enlarge, what you are, in fact, doing is taking something that is scheduled as an interview and turning it into a successful audition. It is a very authentic audition because you are doing you. You are presenting yourself in a heightened fashion. You always know that what you are extending, intensifying, and enlarging comes from what you are already doing or are about to do. And you do it spontaneously! If you coach yourself to enlarge any aspect of who you are, you are enlarging who you are. If you observe your own body feeling while doing this, you will feel the heightened energy. This tool requires that you be fearless. You must find the courage to go for it.

I Am

If you lose your feeling of "I am," just say it to yourself as often as you need to while listening to the interviewer. The "I am" feeling will return to you. It will also return if you tell a new truth or you play Yes! And. . . right after the interviewer says something. Then you will have an opportunity to build a new sequence. If you find yourself off focus or becoming fragmented, just spot it without judging. Then go into telling the truth or Yes! And . . . or relax yourself by coaching "I am" or go into Reflection Listening. These are all tools that can be used midstream.

Tell a Truth

Telling a truth starts you off on a positive focus. The interviewer will be surprised hearing it and will respond to your truth in a neutral or positive fashion, but never with any negativity. You deprive the interviewer of that first negative impression that he or she frequently experiences. The interviewer doesn't have to take care of you or protect him or herself from being manipulated. Every time you start an interview or restart an interview with a truth, you will not get a negative response from the person across the desk. The response may be something like, "Oh, yes, there are file cabinets over there." Or, the interviewer may build on it a bit. Then you will have an open connection or bridge between you that you can build on. If the first line is an impression, opinion, or compliment, it tends to disconnect the other person from you because it feels unsafe.

A first line of truth is safe. It is irrefutable. "That is a green chair." There is no threat inherent. There is no agenda. There is nothing but the truth. It is a safe statement. It is what it is. Whenever you are frantic or panicked, tell another truth. Truth is always the safest place to start because it relaxes the other person. Relaxation in a casting office is very unusual, and the casting director will appreciate this feeling. You will be liked for giving the interviewer a brief respite from the tension that surrounds and infuses these meetings. This tension is a breeding ground for inauthenticity and victimization, which further acts to heighten the tension.

If you want to experience the power of this tool in a social situation, turn to the person next to you, someone whom you don't know, and tell a truth line. Then sit back and watch what happens.

Stay open to exploring different syntax for the truth line. If your truth line always starts with "You've got," pull out the word *you*. Instead, try "There is a hole in your desk." That will open the conversation up.

Looking at Your Résumé

The casting director will never know that you are actively keeping him or her from your résumé. That thought should never surface. If you are creating an experience and the casting director never looks down to your résumé, then you are successful. If not, the casting director will just do what he or she always does when there is no experience to participate in—become a caretaker. In other words, you really hadn't failed because you were receiving the same response that you would have gotten without trying your new interview technique. There is no downside to this process.

Your Progress

You can now give yourself a pat on the back for how much better your interviews are than they were before beginning this work. You are starting to take charge of your meetings. You are being the host. You have the opportunity to play Score to take your transformation further. Score is a wonderful tool for addressing issues such as fear. And as you begin employing Extend, Intensify, and Enlarge as an active focus, it will be natural for you to feel some fear. So keep working, play Score, and see if you can eliminate that fear.

Fine-Tuning

Dorian: I noticed sometimes it seemed like the person who was creating the experience wasn't letting the other person get a word in edgewise. Is that something to avoid doing?

Book: Yes. You can be overbearing, muscling it. Just stay alert. A good host includes the guest. You just have to stay alert and be comfortable with whatever you do. It is possible that as you get the body feeling of "this is working," you like it so much that you start to "muscle" it. Stay alert to feeling that and, if you do, just relax into it and take out the effort.

Mark: Is it accurate to say that if we overplay it a little, they will still get caught up in the experience?

Book: Usually. And sometimes the interviewer will overplay it right back at you, which only means they are really into having the experience with you. They become a willing participant in your improv. When that happens it is very refreshing for them. They are sitting there all day long taking care of one victim after another: "Okay, so you did six weeks of summer stock in Rhode Island . . . ?" So many actors sit waiting to answer questions as if they are being interrogated by cops. It's such a pleasant relief when an actor comes in and doesn't need care. You are always going to get a positive response. The more they get involved in your experience, the more they will say to you, "Hello. This is great. You are wonderful." Their participation becomes more and more effortless. When they join your groove, i.e., "Yes! And . . .," their contributions to the experience get bigger and bigger. The experience between you exponentially grows.

Tracy: What is the difference between telling a truth and giving an opinion you honestly believe in?

Book: An opinion carries more of a visceral, experiential feeling. With an opinion you too easily get caught up in justifying your opinion. That feeling is similar to discovering that you are standing in quicksand. An opinion is as problematic as a compliment. You end up having to justify it. So you are running to catch up, and that is a victim feeling. When you tell a truth it is so clean that you immediately move on. You don't have to justify it.

Dorian: Isn't it possibly bad to end the interview too soon? Maybe they need to talk more with you?

Book: The feedback I get from former students who have adopted this interview approach is, "So, I ended it when it was ended, and I was saying goodbye to leave, and they insisted I stay." If it needs to be longer or should be longer, let them invite you back. Then you know you are doing well. That is only a good feeling. They are the ones who say, "Hey, where are you going? We haven't talked yet. Come back here." What does that mean if they say that? They like you. Always leave them wanting more. Don't self-destruct if you end it early and leave. Don't go out thinking, "Oh, they did not invite me back. They must not like me." That would be a victim's way of thinking. Frequently you go in and you do your two or three minutes, whatever, and boom, you are called the next day to come in for an audition.

Josh: Suppose they ask you a direct question like, "What have you been up to?" You have to talk about your latest projects, don't you?

Book: Don't talk about any projects!

Josh: Won't that seem evasive?

Book: You have no projects to talk about. Josh, let's do an interview right now: "So, what have you been doing, Josh? What's up? What are you working on?"

Josh: I understand what you're saying.

Book: No. Play it out the way you want to play it out. I want to make a point to you. What have you been doing?

Josh: Recently . . . (*Pause*)

Book: Great! That is what you want to share with me?

Josh: No—

Book: That you can't get a job?

Josh: No—

James: Is it different if you are doing something?

Book: Is it on your résumé?

James: I am doing two shows right now, and they're not on my résumé yet.

Book: Why not? It shows you off advantageously, to be currently working, especially in two shows.

James: Okay, but until I make the new résumé, if somebody asks, I should just avoid saying that I am in two shows right now?

Book: No. If it comes up spontaneously, mention it, but don't get bogged down with it. "I am working on *Mother Courage*, and I am doing a spot on *ER*. That is a pink jacket you are wearing." Don't talk about your credits. Your credits are on your résumé. And don't get caught up trying to engineer a conversation so that you can mention them. You would then have a hidden agenda, which would keep you from being present or authentic.

Your credits aren't that great anyway. So, what is there to talk about? You want to help them take time and focus on the fact that you only work on student films or off-off-off Broadway? Where is the sense in that? Are you going to say, "Well I did this part in an AFI film and I had a walk-on on *ER* and an under-five on *Days Of Our Lives*? And I just started rehearsals for a children's theater production?"

Even if they are seeing your résumé for the first time because you brought it with you, they only need fifteen seconds to read it. They are not reading the details. They are just looking to see at what level your career is. It takes them fifteen seconds to know. Talking about any of these gigs is a waste of time and fulfills nothing, except that you may be trying to snow them with credits they have already decided don't make you a money player. When that happens, not only do they dislike your manipulation, but they think you are naive about what your credits really stand for. And if you do have a résumé that is worth talking about, what is there to talk about? It is there in the résumé. Some interviewers will glance at your training history to see where you went to school. Some directors, usually those with theater backgrounds, do this to see if you and he or she speak the same language. Using the same vocabulary makes directing easier.

When I interview actors for my classes, they have already attended a presentation on what my class is about; scheduling the interview with me signifies that they understand what the class is about, feel it is suitable for them, and are applying for admission. I look at the résumé at the beginning of the interview. If the actor has guest-starred on twenty network TV shows, the interview only needs to last five minutes. What is there to talk about? If somebody comes in without that kind of a résumé, I can see that with a quick glance at the résumé. If the person is over forty years old and has the résumé of a twenty-two-year-old, then I want to find out why through seeing him or her audition.

Whether you have a strong or weak résumé, talking about your credits is always a turn-off for the interviewer. If you have a killer résumé and talk about it, you will seem like a braggart; and if you have a weak résumé, why call attention to it? There is nothing to talk about on a résumé unless the actor is a victim whom I have to take care of. In that situation, the résumé provides me with talking points. However, if I am taking care of the victim, the interview is only going to last until I can politely end it.

Your new interview techniques will take the interviewer's attention away from your credits and get him or her to look at you, the person. Actors who come into interviews as victims and think that the interview is all about their résumé—the way you guys all did in the first interview—put the focus on their lack of career success. When you approach it this new way, the focus gets shifted from your career totally onto you as a person.

Laura: Can this interview process be used in other situations, like, in an acquaintance situation? For instance, if someone is in a powerful position in Hollywood, but you are not there for an interview on a business level, can this somehow be used to maneuver it into a business level without being manipulative or wanting something from them?

Book: Since we agree that you should not want something from them, what you are really asking is how to camouflage your wanting something from them?

Laura: Right.

Book: If you meet people socially, which is the premise of your question, it is not a business meeting. If you meet them socially, keep the business out of it. It doesn't mean you can't create an experience. It doesn't mean you cannot exchange phone numbers. It doesn't mean they can't call you in for something if they know you are an actor. It does mean you don't want something from them. *When you want something from people, they know it.* By not wanting something from them, they will like you a whole lot more. However, there is nothing wrong in observing an opportunity as long as you are honest with yourself as to whether or not it is an actual opportunity or a social interaction you want to change into an opportunity. Either way, you can enjoy your chat by not wanting anything. Perhaps in the last ten seconds of the socializing, there is nothing wrong with saying, "You know, I don't have representation right now. Do you think it would be beneficial for us to have a meeting?" If you truly didn't want anything from him or her, that question will get a positive response. The agent will probably say, "Come on in," and if he or she says no, it will probably be said in a supportive fashion. You will walk away feeling good because you took your shot without being a victim or a manipulator.

Practicing your new interview technique will provide you with the tools not to want something from people in positions to further your career and to have experiences with them as equals. In Chapter 8 we will learn a new tool for these kinds of social situations.

Sean: All over this town there are people telling people to want things from people, which is always so uncomfortable; yet there are so many people who seem to think that is the way to go about it, and if you don't go about it that way, you are not going to make it. I have been hearing that for so long, and I never wanted to believe it.

Book: There is a time and place for everything. There is nothing wrong with wanting a career and having a passion for wanting to be an actor. That is one thing. You have to want it and go after it, but there is authentic going after something and there is inauthentic going after something.

Authentically pursuing your career is committing your
time and money to performing in workshops, small theater
productions, student and low-budget films, effective classes,
making rounds, and finding the bravery necessary for changing
your behavior through practicing these interview exercises.
That is authentically going after something. That is brave.
Inauthentically going after something is your using the con,
the seduction, and bullshit.

6

Creating Your Program

Gaining Finesse with Score

Book: Anybody work with Score this week?

Laura: When I started to keep score I noticed that I kept saying things to myself like, "Damn, I did that again. I'm so pathetic," even as I was marking the score. Then I stopped saying these things to myself and just made the mark.

Book: Score works best when you don't put judgment on what you are scoring. Simply do the physical acknowledgment of the behavior by making the tick mark.

Laura: I noticed it was a good feeling to just mark it and not judge it. It made it not such a big deal, and it made it feel somewhat empowering.

Book: Instead of being angry when you have to make a score mark, look at that moment as an opportunity to work on yourself, and, perhaps, be grateful for that opportunity. Gratitude is a much more pleasant feeling than self-put-down. You feel empowered because you are sensing that you are on the path to your goal, and discovering that the path is not difficult. It is obvious to you that the lack of difficulty promises success.

Brian: I was finding that being more aware of victim stuff made it difficult to work with some people. I have been working with someone who is a real victim, and I always get annoyed at him. It dawned on me that if I'm not putting myself down when I'm a victim and just scoring it, perhaps I should just observe it when my co-worker does it and not put him down. Well, doing that has led me to being generous with him instead of being annoyed. It has been so much easier for me to be generous and a much more pleasant experience. Now I think this whole being-annoyed thing was just another victim stance of mine.

Book: Now you have an opportunity to explore that in your journal.

Andrew: My problem is that I am still not aware of when I assume a victim stance. I know I laugh inappropriately sometimes and I have been keeping score of that, but it is never more than three a day, and that dropped to zero pretty fast. So it was very successful in getting me to stop that, but I think there are other manifestations that I'm not aware of.

Book: So your question really is, "How do you know what your victim manifestations are?" Is that right?

Andrew: Yes. I will agree with that, but I think I know the answer.

Book: What is the answer?

Andrew: You feel it.

Book: That's right. When you feel it, what can you do?

Andrew: Make a check.

Book: What else can you do, given that you are talking about not really knowing what the specific manifestations are? What else can you do?

Andrew: Remember the feeling?

Book: More valuable than simply making a check mark every time you have a body sensation of being a victim would be to stop and observe it and track it. If you stop and look at what you did in the moment before you felt the victim body sensation, you will probably find that you engaged in one of the specific behaviors on the list of victim stance and manipulation manifestations. Then you could add that to unnecessary laughing and keep score of it.

Andrew: Then you don't have to worry about changing anything; you just know that when you do that to make a check mark.

Book: Right. One of the common problems with the first time doing Score is that people mistakenly think they are supposed to score every single item on that list. That is inaccurate. There are too many. If you do one behavior a lot, then score that one only. If you do a little or a lot of three behaviors, then you score these three. Avoid scoring more than three. Make sure you designate which ones you are going to score, e.g., unnecessary laughing, lying, and unnecessary apology. That is all you score, the three designated behaviors.

Andrew: Are those the big three?

Book: I don't know what the big three are. Everybody is different.

Tracy: Well, my car got broken into.

Book: Common victim behavior.

Tracy: I felt like such a victim afterward. Then I felt really needy and I didn't want to be by myself. I didn't know if I should mark that down. Am I being needy, or is this just unnecessary?

Book: Had you, previous to that occasion, decided feeling needy was something that you were going to keep score on?

Tracy: That was one of them.

Book: Then, yes, you could, and it would have been appropriate. How many behaviors did you pick off the list that you chose to score?

Tracy: I don't know the number. I just said, "I do these things."

Book: So, you are in the same boat that Andrew is.

Tracy: I need to be more specific.

Book: Yes. You only pick one, two, or three behaviors. I recently played Score myself to clean up a particular bad habit. I just scored one thing, one specific thing. That is all you can do. One, two, three at the most. Specific items. You are not scoring victim-with-a-capital-V behavior. You are scoring every time you (fill in the blank): "Feel needy" for Tracy, "Laughs at things that are not funny" for Andrew. Whatever yours are, just score that. Forget the word *victim*. Remove it from the whole process. Forget large issues for Score. Pick very specific and unambiguous behaviors— "unnecessary apologies." You can even do it over other issues, e.g., eating when not hungry. You pick whatever it is and be specific. To get started, I suggest picking only one thing and not three.

Anthony: I was keeping score of how often I get angry. This morning my car wouldn't start and instead of reacting with anger, I felt the anger begin and I immediately scored it.

I noticed the anger went away and I just went about the business of getting the car fixed.

Book: Exactly. Anger is a feeling and it isn't on our list, but it adversely affected your behavior and you wanted to address that.

James: My issue was arguing with myself on whether something should be scored.

Book: Can you give me an example of what one of these arguments sounded like?

James: I was keeping score of every time I told a lie. Sometimes, I would get confused between a lie and a white lie. I wasn't really lying, but then I would come back and go, "Yeah, but you did lie." I was not really sure what to do. I would go back and forth between was it a lie or wasn't it.

Book: And up to this point you hadn't taken the score?

James: No.

Book: And you're still deliberating?

James: Yes.

Book: Save yourself the aggravation. If you wonder if maybe you should score something, go ahead and score it.

Linda: Should I select a designated hour to do it or should I wait till some spontaneous moment during the day and say, "Oh, I'm going to start my hour right now?"

Book: In the beginning, designate a specific time period and commit to keeping score during that period—keep that appointment.

Christina: I would select a specific time and forget to do it. The next day I would even write it in my appointment book, but still forget to do it.

Book: Despite the fact that you planned to do it and made the appointment with yourself in your appointment book, you still didn't choose to do it. When you choose to keep score, you will find yourself anticipating the start of your designated appointment to do it. That will be your proof to yourself that you have chosen to do it.

Dorian: I chose two things to score and I did it two hours a day.

Book: Were you "on it" for two hours? Were you diligent?

Dorian: There were times when I faded out, and I reminded myself.

Book: How long were your fade-out periods?

Dorian: Ten minutes here; ten minutes there.

Book: It seems like your initial time periods for playing Score were too long. In the beginning, select an amount of time that will allow you to be one-hundred percent diligent. After you get used to being one-hundred percent diligent you can stretch your time periods for playing. So the second day, how long were you on it?

Dorian: I did it for two hours again and every day for a week.

Book: When did you quit?

Dorian: You know, I didn't notice or score anything the last two days.

Book: Hello.

Dorian: So I can have faith in that, or does that mean that it was a fluke?

Book: You may have just discovered a new victim manifestation that you can score: self-diminishment, not taking credit for having done something. The bottom line is that you chose to play Score on some self-limiting behavior and after one week the behavior has disappeared.

Dorian: True, and I have a question about that. One of the other things that I observed was that the situations that

I found myself in this week are situations in which I feel very confident. I am looking forward to situations where I don't necessarily feel so confident. I haven't had those opportunities yet.

Book: What's the question?

Dorian: Will the behavior return when I am in a high-pressure situation?

Book: Right now, you have removed the behavior. Perhaps, in a high-pressure situation, you will discover that you have built up the necessary self-awareness to keep it out at that time also. If not, you will find the bravery to play Score at that time, even while you are under pressure.

Josh: Now that we are noticing and spotting the behaviors, what if we find ourselves inclined to do something about them? Should we avoid that? That seems to be the whole point of the exercise.

Book: Are you talking about after you stop playing Score?

Josh: No. As you are playing Score, if you find yourself about to do or say something that you are scoring, and you catch it before you do it, should you not do it or do it and score it?

Book: If at the moment that you are about to do something that you don't like yourself doing, and you choose not to do it, that is called progress. It is called self-awareness and taking responsibility for your behavior. Suppose you are on vacation and you meet a woman, and you are schmoozing, and you find yourself "showing off." It feels inauthentic and you choose to keep score whenever you "show off." By the end of your vacation (and scorekeeping) week, you are in a bar and you meet this nice woman, and you find yourself about to do a showoff thing, and you spot it before you are about to do it and you say to yourself, "I am not going to do that." Then you continue the conversation with her with

out showing off. That is what we are after. That is called
changing behavior. You don't have to do anything but set out
to keep score when you are playing Score. In time, you won't
even have that mid-step of consciously spotting that you
are about to do something. In time, the impulse to do that
something gets removed altogether.

Wayne: I played Score while I was at my day job. I worked for
four days and was off for two, so I chose my time periods to
match my shifts. I felt more inauthentic than ever, because
I was noticing that I felt like I was "on." I was laughing at
people's stupid jokes.

Book: What were you choosing to score?

Wayne: Laughter, nervousness—those two.

Book: Just two items.

Wayne: Yes.

Book: How long did you choose to play Score for on the first
day?

Wayne: As I said, five-thirty until eleven o'clock.

Book: Five and a half hours; that is the equivalent of some
very fat person saying to him or herself, "Goddamn it, I am
so serious about changing my life and losing weight. So,
you know what I am going to do tomorrow? I am going
to commence a diet in which I don't eat a thing for three
months." How realistic is that?

Wayne: I didn't think of it like that.

Book: I know you didn't. There is an importance to playing
by the rules. In the introduction to Score, you were told
ten minutes the first day, twenty minutes, an hour tops. You
jumped in at five-and-a-half hours. Do it for ten minutes
a day, fifteen minutes the third day, and a half-hour the
second week. Just do it in short increments. You won't be
overwhelmed by how much you do your stuff. How much

can you do in ten minutes? Build up some credibility with yourself instead of building up the awesomeness of the challenge. That is what you do when you start out with five or six hours straight. How can you possibly be diligent about playing for five-and-a-half hours when you have no practice at being self-aware for even a half hour? It can be done if you work your way up to it. But, guess what? You won't have to. The success of the process occurs fairly quickly. Dorian did it in a week. Just pick one, two, or three behaviors tops and start with short timespans. Be diligent with them. If you can't be diligent with that timespan, make the timespan shorter so you can be diligent with that.

Shannon: I did two hours a day, three things, for six days. By the end of the week I wasn't doing two of the things.

Book: Have the scores of the other thing diminished?

Shannon: Yes.

Book: Then extend the time you play, be diligent, and it will disappear very quickly.

Veronica: I had a gig this week and I noticed that on the set that I tend to have a lot of anxiety: the whole movie-making, acting, show business, stars, director, producers, crew, etcetera. There is a lot of victim behavior going on, on the set. It seems like the crew almost expects it from the actors. After playing Score for a few days, I could see the difference in my behavior. I could also see a difference in the other people. They started treating me differently. I felt they cared about me, whereas, before, I never had that feeling.

Book: They probably didn't care about you while you were being inauthentic or acting as a victim. Removing your victim and manipulation manifestations transforms you and that transformation is very appealing. When you see a positive change in how people treat you, you know you are on the right track.

Lisa: I have two things that I do a lot.

Book: You picked two behaviors that you do a lot. What time period did you give yourself?

Lisa: Ten minutes.

Book: Did you play for those ten minutes?

Lisa: Yes.

Book: Second day?

Lisa: Second day it was fifteen minutes.

Book: Did you play for the full fifteen minutes?

Lisa: Yes.

Book: The third day?

Lisa: The third day I got up to half an hour and the scorecard started getting worse.

Book: And what happened next?

Lisa: By the end of the week, Saturday was a bad day—I did an hour and I got an eight. Sunday, I started not doing the behavior. I could feel myself saying, "Stop!" before I would do it. Today I played Score again and my score was zero again.

Book: Isn't that a major success?

Lisa: I guess. It took me all week to do it.

Book: Come on.

Lisa: Okay, it is a success story.

Book: Did you see how, when we were talking with Dorian, how she wouldn't take credit for what she was doing? Now you are doing that, too.

Lisa: I am a victim!

Book: Are you?

Lisa: Yes.

Book: Do you know how long you have to go to a shrink and pay huge amounts of money to change a piece of behavior, if you are lucky and it even changes?

Lisa: A long time.

Book: You did it in a week, and notice, Lisa, that you are complaining that it took a whole week. Notice that. There is something that you can write about in your journal.

Mark: I would always forget to carry a scorecard and I found that I could keep score by pulling on my spiral watchband.

Book: Did you transfer your score to a home scorecard?

Mark: No.

Book: Did you notice any change in your behavior or your scores?

Mark: No.

Book: Snapping a watch or rubber band on your wrist is as ineffective as substituting a deliberate cough instead of writing your score. These scoring approaches will greatly diminish the effectiveness of the tool because your score disappears after you "mark" it. The sound of the cough disappears with the wind. There is no record of the number of watchband snaps at the end of the day. A scorecard should be permanent and in the space, not your head. It must be there. It is on paper and it is on the home board. If you are going to improvise your own version of keeping score, pick one where the score doesn't disappear.

Krista: Do we have to say, "Tuesday I am going to do this between one and one-fifteen," or can you say, "When I find myself in that situation, e.g., when I am with a bunch of people, I will do it for the next ten minutes and notice my behavior?"

Book: I doubt it would be successful if you designate your time period by saying, "When I am in that situation," because when you are in that situation, you are not going to think to start it. Understand the concept and commit to a short period of time in which you are one-hundred percent diligent. Do it every day, and it won't take long. How much more reasonable can you get?

Additional Benefits

After playing Score for a while, you should find that, in addition to cleaning up the negative behaviors you are scoring, you are becoming more self-aware. This should be especially noticeable to you when you are interacting with another person. You will become more alert to energy drops between the two of you, which in a social situation is the equivalent of the interviewer's head dropping to read your résumé. But you should perceive the drop before the energy is completely depleted. When that perception occurs, you can heighten the energy flow between the two of you and prevent "the head drop." Just extend that thought, enlarge that gesture, intensify that sound, which should compel the person's attention back to you.

As your awareness increases, you may become more frustrated and annoyed with certain people. Increasing your self-awareness brings about a higher degree of honesty. You will more easily identify inauthenticity and victim stances in others. You may decide that your relationship with a friend is diminishing you, that you are always taking care of him or her. You may even come to the time that you don't want to be this person's friend any longer.

On the other hand, you might appreciate meeting new people. You might be more likely to see honesty and authenticity in them, and that might be appealing.

Your Journal and Your Program

If you want to deepen the effects of your increasing self-awareness, you may consider *creating a program* for yourself. Your program already has two components with which you are familiar. The first component is playing Score. The second is the use of a journal. Keeping a personal journal will increase your self-awareness to see more clearly what is real and honest. The journal will assist you to continue breaking through your self-imposed limitations, such as your victim stance or inauthenticity.

How Do You Use Your Journal?

Some people make notes of important events from each day and how they handled them. Others write stream-of-consciousness. Still others keep track of behavioral moments of which they are proud, acknowledging what they are doing well. Another form of journal-entrying is recording what happens without commentary and then writing a second page with commentary. It may be as simple as, "I wasn't on focus in today's interview." Continuing this you might say, "Why wasn't I on focus? What was I doing instead? What was I thinking about?" Do this and see where it leads. Some journal entries can be in dialogue form, i.e., an imagined conversation between you and someone else or between you and the issue you are working on. Another journal approach is to change your form of entry from time to time. It can be very healthy and exciting to explore new forms of making entries in your journal.

If you think you have valid reasons for not writing in a journal, you should look at your reasons and consider the possibility that they are lies. A common reason for not doing journal work is the fear of someone's reading it. That is a lie because who is going to read it if it is locked up in your house?

After completing a journal entry, you should ask the question, "Where is the lie in what I just wrote?" This requires reading the journal entry with the express purpose of spotting any lies you may inadvertently have told yourself. If any lies are found, and they will be, you have the opportunity to correct them, and to write about the lies. You can't employ "Where is the lie?" without reading your journal entries. Frequent use of this tool greatly increases your self-awareness and authenticity. If you don't read what you wrote, you are going to assume it is the truth. Here is a sample journal entry:

> I just got home. Today was terrible. I am very angry, so I am writing in my journal because something is going on and I don't know what it is. When did I start getting angry? What happened? I got angry when that dopey secretary in the casting office said blah, blah, blah to me. Then I went in and I really screwed up my audition. Blah, blah, blah and it is all that dope's fault for saying what she said to me in the office. It really got me upset and blah, blah, blah, blah. Where is the lie in what I just wrote?

Then you go back and read the entry, and you should spot the line "It's all that dope's fault" as being a lie. Now the second part of your entry might look like this:

> The lie in what I just wrote was saying, "It's all that dope's fault." I have to take responsibility for myself. I could have seen what she was doing. I could have recognized it. I could have seen that she was pressing my buttons. So, I am not really angry with the secretary. I am not angry at lousing up the audition. I am angry with myself because I allowed my buttons to be pushed.

You could end the entry there or write more about the issues of your buttons being pushed. When using this tool you will probably find lies to write about. But if you have been diligent in reading your entry and still find no lies, answer the question "Where is the lie?" with "I can't find one." Sometimes the lie will hit you later. So then you should go back and write about it.

It is best to avoid putting yourself down in any journal entry; e.g., "I'm such a jerk." Remove the put-down and simply write about the experience. "I notice that I didn't follow through on my impulse. There we were in the interview, and I got an impulse to talk about the sculpture that was in the office and I didn't. I held it in because I thought I wouldn't have anything intelligent to say about it. I don't like it when I do that." Continuing in this fashion may lead you to, "I don't like it when I do that. I wonder why I do that because, up to a point, I thought we were really grooving along. Then I wanted to talk about the sculpture, but all of a sudden, I became afraid. Why? At what point did fear take over? Can I remember? You know, it was when the casting director touched my shoulder when he brought me the coffee. I got nervous. Isn't that interesting. That is when the fear came in." End of entry.

Then for insurance sake, start the next entry, "Where is the lie in what I just wrote?"

Another journal tool that can take you deeper into your work on yourself is to start a journal entry with *"When did I start becoming a victim?"* Or you could ask it in another way: "When did my childlike optimism change?" Nobody was born as a victim. When did your childlike optimism change so that you became a victim? Then just start writing about that. When you are finished, then ask, "Where is the lie in what I just wrote?"

There is a lot to write about. The more you write about your behavior, feelings, thoughts, and observations, the more aware you will become. Change without awareness is impossible. When you use your journal, you commit to working on yourself. Anyone can ruminate on his or her problems, but to choose to write about them, that is commitment. Additionally, Jack Lee Rosenberg and Beverly Kitaen-Morse elaborate, "Writing in a journal involves your body with your mind and provides a perspective that allows you to witness and examine your interior life."[1] Avoid using a computer, and use a journal with no lines on the pages so that you can write more spontaneously and even draw pictures. Use a flowing ink pen like a fountain, gel, or Uniball pen. Avoid a regular ballpoint pen. The unlined paper and a pen with ink that flows easily enhance a freer form of writing that encourages your stream of consciousness to flow. A ballpoint pen is really uptight and doesn't flow as easily.

Journal work and playing Score are two components of a *program* to address these issues. You have other options available: *meditating, prayer*, even *abstinence*. Adding any of these practices to your journal work, to your keeping score, and your other new tools, will create a personalized program for getting rid of the behaviors that you do not like in yourself. Journal work is a lifelong process.

7

BOUNDARIES

More and more you are now becoming your authentic self. As this occurs, you may become conscious of your boundaries for the first time. "Boundaries are the energetic limits of the Self. A Self boundary is the sense (or experience or awareness) of the Self that is separate from the world, yet exists in harmonious relationship with it. It is flexible, so that others can be allowed closer in at will or be kept further out."[1] Authentic Self boundaries are different from defense-system boundaries, which are rigid and developed to keep others out in order to protect the Self.

Here is a character-creating acting focus from Improvisation Technique that will allow you to experience your boundaries.

Extension Bumps[2]

Setup

This exercise, which introduces the concept of boundaries, is best practiced with at least one other person. If you cannot do this, then you may want to try it out at a social gathering or in a large store or market. The exercise will, of course, have to be modified, but it can be done.

Warm-Up Exercises

Stand still and take forty breaths, pausing briefly between each set of ten. Keep your eyes open. The breaths should be big ones, not slowly done, but not rushed. Draw them in and out through your mouth and into your chest, with an emphasis on the inhale and a relaxed exhale. Right after the last breath, look around the room and identify objects by naming them by their colors.

You will, of course, do the naming silently if you are in a crowd of strangers or near strangers: "There is a blue clock; she is wearing a green sweater; that is a black chair." When naming the colors/ objects, you must focus and commit to the naming.

Extension Bumps Exercise

Allow about ten to thirty seconds to experience each change of focus. As you walk around, focus on feeling the space you are moving through. Keep your eyes open. Change your focus and feel the space moving through you. Next, focus on moving through the space and feeling the space move through you at the same time. Here's a brand-new focus—see any other people. Then, focus on letting them see you. Change your focus and see them and let them see you at the same time. Change your focus again and feel yourself at the center of your own space as you walk. You are at the center of your space, which extends out in all directions and travels with you wherever you go. Get a sense of how much your space extends out from you. Stay in the center of your own space and take all you need. There is enough room for all to have their own extensions of space. Your space is your own, and no one can come into it unless he or she is invited in. Feel that. There is no right or wrong amount of space available to you. It is what you feel comfortable with. Continue walking and focus on seeing the other people and avoiding their extensions of space. Sense or see the space around others and feel the space around you, low and high. Avoid each other's space extensions. Be aware that every person is at the center of his or her own space. Avoid bumping into another player's space with yours.

After a few minutes, bump space extensions—not bodies, just space extensions. Keep your body quiet at the center of your own space. Only your space is bumping into another's space. Let the space extensions bump and collide. Stay open to any feeling that arises. Avoid acting out the bumping. Your body doesn't need to do anything, except be open to feelings; it's the space that's bumping. Let your body experience whatever it experiences. Keep bumping or colliding space extensions as you pass one another. After a few minutes, stop bumping and continue walking. Let go of your space extensions. Go through the space of the room and let the space go through you.

Follow-Up Questions

Did you feel your own space extension?

Did you know where it ended?

How did it feel being at the center of your own space?

When your extension bumped into another's, where in your body did you feel it?

What did you feel?

Were you capable of feeling without acting it out, without performing the feeling?

Summary

In your personal lives, you experience space extensions without being conscious of them. They are called *boundaries*. When somebody comes into your space, that person crosses your boundary. How does that feel? How did you feel when that happened during the space extension bumps? Irritated. Aggressive. Claustrophobic. Sad. Threatened. What else? These are all negative feelings, which is what happens when somebody crosses your boundaries. Another word for what you feel is *inundated*. You feel inundated when another person moves in on you. Whenever someone crosses your boundary, you feel violated.

It is your space, no matter the size. Whatever it is, if you focus on your own boundaries and establish what they are, you will be respected and you will feel safe.

You may not have ever thought about your boundaries before, but you certainly knew when you were inundated. Think of some stranger coming up to you in a bar or on the street and getting just a little too close. Remember how you felt when your mother went through your dresser drawers when you were a child or teenager? How about when a teacher or employer got in your face? Sometimes, comments that certain people say to you are just a little too personal, and that feels inundating. Some interviewers (casting directors, producers, directors, agents, or managers) will unintentionally or intentionally cross your boundaries and provoke you. They may comment on your lack of success or your physical appearance or inquire into your personal life or be rude. At these times, you can have an authentic response to being inundated, which is healthy, or you can act out your response to inundation, which is inauthentic and not healthy. Inauthentic acting out will probably take the form of being a victim or a manipulator. You won't be called back. Authentic responses to being inundated usually take the form of creating breathing room for yourself, taking a break, going to the restroom, feeling free not to talk about private issues, and never saying yes when you mean no.

Here is another exercise for getting better in touch with your boundaries. It will supply you with an acting focus tool that may be helpful at interviews.

Boundary Walls[3]

Setup

Two people are needed to do this exercise. You will benefit from just reading the exercise, but working with a partner will help you to discover more. You will either be assigned number one or number two. If you are a "one" you sit in an open part of the room, not near a wall. If you are a "two" you stand, but as far away from your partner as the room will allow.

Rules

Number two, slowly walk toward your seated partner. Number one, when you feel your partner is getting too close, say *stop*. Put your finger on the floor at the spot your partner's feet stopped. If you have to leave your seated position to put your finger on the floor, do so. Number two, move away. Number one, where you are pointing is a spot on the circumference of a circle you will now draw with your finger on the floor around you and your chair. Your chair will be at the center of the circle. When you have finished drawing the circle, physically make contact with a circular space wall extending up from your floor circle. With open palms feel your space wall, high and low, all around you. Allow time for this.

Return to your chair when you are finished. Inside this wall, your boundary, you are safe. Address number two by name and tell him or her, "This is my space and you may not come in unless I invite you." Number two, walk in again from a different angle. One, say *stop* again when your partner gets to your boundary wall. At that time, two, move away. You can use your boundary to keep out anything: actions, people, or words. Now reverse roles.

Follow-Up Questions

What did you feel when it was time to say *stop* the first time?

Where in your body did you feel it?

What were or are some of the things you wanted to keep out?

What did you feel when it was time to say *stop* the second time?

Where in your body did you feel it?

When you were inside your boundary wall or space, what did you feel?

Where in your body did you feel it?

How did it feel when you said, "This is my space and you may not come in unless I invite you?"

Summary

Prior to an interview, physicalize your space wall boundary and trust that you can use it to keep out anything that you don't want to let in. Boundaries can be effective in keeping out physical closeness, words, negativity, judgment, or fear. You may not feel comfortable doing it in the waiting room before an interview, but you certainly could do it at home before you leave, in your car, the parking lot, or a restroom. Physicalizing the space wall instead of imagining it is important because you are making a real commitment to knowing and creating your boundary. What is imagined in your head is too easily forgotten. Having a physical connection to your boundary's location heightens your ability to recognize when it has been crossed. That higher consciousness also allows you to choose not to react in an inauthentic fashion. A mature and powerful adult replaces the angry or fearful child.

Doing this exercise will also enhance your respect for the interviewer's boundaries—something you may have never considered. Casting director Kim Nordlinger (*The X Files*; *Sabrina, the Teenage Witch*) talks about this in reference to audition behavior, and it is just as true for interviews: "If the audition sides call for a touch or romantic interlude with the other character, you'll need to find some creative way to suggest that action without invading the casting director's or reader's personal space. This may seem obvious, but you'd be surprised how many actors will reach out and try to grab my hand or attempt to caress my face during an audition. That's just not appropriate. It breaks everyone's concentration. There's no need for it and it doesn't enhance your performance."[4]

8

The Witness

I f you were capable of watching your interviews while you were doing them, what would you see, and could you do anything with that information while you continued with the interview? For the final level of our interview technique, we will develop a tool that allows us to be our authentic selves while simultaneously creating an experience and witnessing the process. The ability to be a witness has many benefits that we will explore.

Introductory Witness Walk[1]

Setup

You may, of course, just read through this exercise, but you will benefit more if you do the exercise with a partner. The complete introductory witness walk takes about forty minutes.

Rules

Your partner will guide or coach you through the exercise first. Then you will switch and you will be the coach. All the coach has to do is read the exercise out loud starting with the next paragraph— follow the suggested time allotments that appear in brackets (don't read them out loud). Your participation is nonverbal; you are simply to respond to the coaching. If you do not understand something, let it go. It should be clarified through subsequent coaching. Do not spend time attempting to figure out any coaching.

Introductory Witness-Walk Exercise

Walk around. Keep your eyes open. Explore what it means to focus. While you walk, respond to the coaching. Just put your focus on what you are coached to do. [Allow two to five seconds between coaching sentences.] As you walk around, focus on feeling the floor with your feet. Now change the focus and allow the floor to feel your feet. It's a new focus. Let the floor feel your feet. Keep walking naturally. Don't slide your feet. Go back to the first focus, feel the floor with your feet. Change the focus again and allow the floor to feel your feet.

Here's a brand-new focus—keep walking and feel the floor with your feet and let the floor feel your feet at the same time. *Focusing means giving your full body attention to the exercise, excluding any distractions.* Feel your toes with your toes. Feel the arches of your feet. Feel the skin on the top of the bone. Feel your heels. Feel your ankles with your ankles. Go up your leg and feel the bones of your leg.

You are feeling your skeleton with your skeleton. You have the opportunity to feel your skeleton instead of visualizing it. Keep walking. Now, put space where the bones are. Feel your knee joints. Feel the skin over your knee joints and let your knee joints feel the skin and the flesh. Now, put space where your knee joints are. Feel your clothes against your legs and let your legs feel the clothes. Feel your underclothing against your body and let your body feel your underclothing. Feel the pelvic area. Feel your genitals. Put space where they are. Feel your lower belly. Go up to your rib cage and feel the rib cage with the rib cage. Feel your clothes on top of your chest, on your arms. Let your chest and arms feel the clothes. Let the clothes feel the chest. Let your head rest on its own pedestal. Neither pull it back nor pull it down. Let it do what it will. Keep walking.

Move into your face now and feel your cheeks. Feel your mouth. Let your cheeks feel your mouth and your mouth feel your cheeks at the same time. Go inside your nose and into your ear canal. Go into the ear canal and observe any obstacle that might be in there or any discomfort or any deadness. Go behind your eyes and feel the lids over your eyes and let your lids feel the eyes. Let your eyes feel the lids. Feel your forehead and allow your forehead to be free of censoring you. Keep walking.

Go inside your face and see if you can feel the expression of your face from the inside. Anyone who can feel it, see if you can alter the expression on your face from the inside. If you don't feel it, it is not necessary to change it. Feel the hair on your head and let your head feel the hair. Now feel the space above you and feel the space behind you. Feel the space under your feet, the space between your fingers. Become the space and don't worry about what that means. You just do it, or don't do it.

Close your eyes and stop walking. When you open your eyes, you will be in a new space, a new place. You are still in the same room, but it will be new, as if you have never been here before. It is brand-new. Do not visualize another room. Open your eyes and see the new place you are in. [Allow ten seconds.]

Now, walk around in *this* new place. Keep seeing it as you walk in it. [Allow ten seconds.] Stop and close your eyes. When you open your eyes, you will be in still another new place. Open your eyes. See this new place that you are in. Don't walk yet, just take it all in. Allow ten seconds. Now, walk around in *this* new place. Keep seeing it as you walk in it. [Allow ten seconds.] Stop and close your eyes. When you open your eyes, you will be in still another new place. Open your eyes. See this new place that you are in. Don't walk yet, just take it all in. [Allow five seconds.] Now, take a step into this new and unknown place. Now, with the *next* step you take, go into still another new and unknown place. Take another step into still another new and unknown place.

Now keep taking the next step, and each step that you take goes someplace new and unknown, someplace that you have never been before. With each step you take, go into a new and unknown place. Take normal-size steps. [Allow about one and a half minutes.] Now, start to decrease the amount of time you take between the steps. Spend less time in each new and unknown place. You are decreasing the amount of time between the steps, but with every step you take, you still go into a new and unknown place. Eventually you will decrease the time between the steps until you are simply walking normally without time between steps. Avoid playing safe. The essence of the unknown implies risk. Get to the point where you are walking at a normal pace and let your focus go to a new and unknown place with every step. An observer would say that you were just walking, but you know that with every step you are going to a new and different place.

See the sights around you in each new place. ***Take a ride on your body*** and view the sights that keep changing with each new step. You are open to seeing whatever reveals itself to you. Your body is walking, and you are taking a ride on your own body to unknown places. [Allow thirty seconds.]

Change your focus so you just feel the space you walk through and feel the space go through you. [Allow thirty seconds.] With the next step you take, step into the space and then step back out of it, leaving your body impression in the space in front of you. Now, look at your body impression in the space. Walk around it and look at it. [Allow fifteen seconds.] Feel your body's impression in the space. Avoid judging it, just feel all the parts of it. [Allow one minute.] Now, pick up your space body. Put it on your shoulders, piggyback style. Walk around. It is made of space, so it doesn't weigh anything. You are carrying it around the room, so in fact, your space body is taking a ride on your real body. You're doing the work and the space body is doing nothing; it is simply taking a ride on your body. [Allow ten seconds.] Now shift your focus in order to see through the space body's eyes instead of your own. Do the best you can. Get the feeling of seeing all the sights around you from the space eyes above you. Allow your real arms to swing naturally. Keep seeing through your space body's eyes above you. Stay open to this feeling: of seeing from above you. Take a ride on your own body. See all the sights around you. [Allow one minute for this.]

Now, stop and set your space body down on its feet and face it. Now, take the arms of the space body and just raise them and lower them so that the arms are rotating from the sockets. You raise them up and lower them—not out to the sides—just up and down. As you do this, watch the space arms going up and down. Do not bend either your elbows or the space elbows. Keep watching them go up and down. [Allow twenty seconds for this.]

Now, immediately shift your focus to your own real arms going up and down and see the trails of your arms, like a series of still pictures. The space arms and body disappear as you see the trails of your real arms, the ghosting of your arms, as they go up and down. [Allow thirty seconds for this.] The trails are in the space in front of you, not in your head. The ghosting is in front of you, not in your head. [Allow fifteen seconds for this.]

Now, raise and lower your arms, in a series of still pictures or moments so that your arms move a little bit and stop—move a little bit and stop. Watch your arms do this. You begin to open to the feeling of being a *witness*, a feeling similar to a ***feeling of doing nothing***. You're doing nothing as your arms move up and down. Focus on doing nothing. It is as if you are staying out of it. [Allow twenty seconds.]

Continue what you are doing, but don't have any stopping points. Raise and lower your arms fluidly, yet maintain the same witness focus. Perhaps it will help if you focus on the places where the stop points had been. If it helps, do it with one arm only. [Allow thirty seconds.] Keep the same exact focus now and allow your arms to raise and lower in triple speed, but keep your focus in normal speed. Don't triple speed your focus because you are staying out of it. Your arms are going up and down in triple speed, but the witness is in normal speed. You are doing nothing. Try this approach: You are observing your arms as if they are not your arms. These arms are strange arms going up and down as you focus on being a witness. Now allow the arms to change to normal speed. You're focusing on being a witness, and your arms are raising and lowering themselves fluidly. [Allow ten seconds.]

Let's extend this to your whole body. Let your body take over from what your arms are doing. You still focus on being a witness. We are now going to substitute the whole body for the arms. Walk around the room as a witness. Focus on the periods of being a witness while you are walking around the room. You stay out of the walking—allow your body to walk without you. Maintain the same exact focus of the witness. [Allow thirty seconds for this.]

Maintain the same focus and allow your body to move at triple speed without your doing anything. You are taking a ride on your own body, so stay out of it. It may feel as if you are continuously falling out of your own body. [Allow fifteen seconds.] Allow your body to return to normal speed without your involvement. Your body is changing speed and you are staying out of it. You are doing nothing as your body changes its own speed. While you are doing nothing, you are free to observe from above, or witness, all the sights around you. The focus is to be a witness. Let your body walk around, and feel free to stay out of it. You are up on top, taking a ride on your own body. It is a feeling similar to that which you experienced when you looked through your space body's eyes above you. View the sights around you. It is also a feeling similar to discovering you are in a new place with every step you take. Witness the new sights. Your body is doing the walking and you are taking a ride as a witness. [Allow thirty seconds.]

While you are on this focus, allow your body to try different activities—sitting and getting up, going up and down stairs, taking and replacing items from your bag, exercising, or doing any activity with space or real props—but stay on the focus of being a witness. While you are up there taking a ride on your body, witnessing, you can witness yourself doing the activity. Your body is free to switch to new activities at any time. Let it happen. There is no effort and it is relaxing. The body is doing it all and you are taking a ride, watching. You are focused on being the witness and discovering that you don't have to focus on the activity, the doing, or the exercise you have selected—your body will do that for you. You are just watching your body do it. That is what it means to be a witness. [Allow three minutes for this activity.] Now come out of it.

Summary

Did you have any moments of experiencing the witness? Did you ever feel that you didn't need to watch where you were walking because your body would just go where it had to go? It is a common understanding that when you are onstage or in front of a camera, about ten percent of your brain is responsible for taking care of you and the rest can be in character. That is partly what this feels like. It is focused, yet relaxed, and at the same time, the part that is observing, the witness, is the same part that allows you to hit your marks or keeps you from stumbling into the orchestra pit.

You are totally at ease while you feel you are doing nothing and have no need to do anything. It is similar to feeling you have nothing at stake. Being a witness means allowing your body to do what it wants or needs to do without your assistance. When you are a witness you stay out of your own way as you take a vacation and enjoy the sights around you. This results in increased clarity and involvement with the environment.

———

There are two occasions other than interviewing when you can practice your new interview technique. The first is any social situation, in which you come into contact with people who are in positions to further your career—this is called *schmoozing*. The second occasion begins at the moment that you walk into a room for an audition and ends when you start the audition. It picks up again after you finish your audition but before you leave the room. These two periods are also schmoozing periods. Everything you have been working on to improve your interviews is relevant to these times also. It is not uncommon for an actor to be selected for a part immediately after an audition, only to lose the part in the schmoozing period following the audition. *What's relevant in an interview is also relevant for all networking and audition schmoozing periods.*

The Schmoozing Witness

You may benefit from reading the next exercise, but you will learn more by participating in it with a friend or fellow actor.

Setup

Choose to become either a "one" or a "two." If you are a "one," select a character for yourself who is in a position to boost an actor's career, e.g., casting director, agent, producer, manager, or director. Your character is defined by your occupational choice. If you are a "two," you will be yourself. You are going to be exactly who you are, no acting choices at all. You will play through this once, switch roles, and play again.

Warm-Up Exercise

"Two," walk around and shake out your body. Turn on your focus. Focus on feeling the space you are walking through and feeling the space moving through you. Now, take a ride on your own body. Walk as a witness with no sense of urgency. Your body is doing the walking and you are taking a ride on your own body. Now, while you are a witness, view the sights around you. You are free. You have the time to see them because you are not doing anything.

Now, with your next step see that you are in a brand-new place. While you are a witness, look around and see everything in this new place for the first time. You have never seen it before. It is all brand-new. You are up on top watching everything. While you are taking in the sights, see your fellow player as one of the sights. Now, see your fellow player as someone who may be in a position to help your career. Witness your fellow player.

First Improv

If you are a "one," set up a living room. A couch, made of three chairs, is to the right. Two chairs facing each other are to your left. In front of you is a space buffet table with food and behind you is a space bar. The wall behind the bar consists of bookcases and a fireplace.

If you are a "two," you are still in the witness mode, still walking around. "One," your part in the improv is to represent the kind of "power people" actors encounter in Hollywood or New York in social situations. This is a show-biz party! Both "one" and "two," you are strangers to each other.

Acting Focus

From here on, "two," your acting focus is to maintain your witness mode as you network and schmooze. All business potential is to be seen from your witness place. Allow your body to employ all the interview tools as it sees fit. You just witness it from above. Stay in the witness. You are yourself, and your focus is to stay in your witness. If you find your witness slipping, coach yourself back into it.

"One," your focus is to play your character. Let the party begin. Continue for approximately fifteen minutes before reversing roles for the second improv.

Second Improv

Warm-Up Exercise and Acting Focus

Don't say anything. Just reverse roles. One, do the witness warm-up from the first improv. Walk in your witness mode. Take all the time you need. It is important that you get a sense that you are a witness and you can sustain it throughout the exercise. Now take a ride on your own body and view the living room at this party.

"Two," choose an occupation for yourself. Are you a director, a producer, a manager, an agent? You are to represent the kind of power people actors encounter in social situations in Hollywood or New York. "One," you are yourself at this party and you are to stay in your witness mode. Begin the party.

Summary

When you were the actor, what did you observe from your witness? Were you able to stay in your witness? Half the time? Some of the time? Not at all? If you had difficulty staying in your witness, were you aware of it and did you experiment with coaching yourself to get into your witness? An excellent way to get into or stay in your witness is the arm-raising sequence from the introductory witness walk (witnessing your arm moving in stop-and-go still pictures and then moving it in fluid motion). You can practice your schmoozing witness at a real party where you have the opportunity to mingle with multiple guests.

Finding Your Power

Frequent responses to the Schmoozing Witness improvs will include:

- I felt better able to take control of a situation. Normally in those situations I feel fear and my victim stuff; this time that all dissipated.

- It felt effortless and confident. I felt more confident and sure of myself without having to work hard at it.

- Usually in this type of situation I feel that I want something from the other person and also that I am being perceived negatively. This time I never felt that way at all. It took that away.

- Better listening overall, and better shaping of my own conversation because there was just an overview. I just got to see a bigger picture.

- I felt just a lot more comfortable in my body and confident. When I thought about it later I realized that being in the witness helped me drop the defense-system boundary I had put on myself, which kept people out. Being in the witness made me more confident and made it so much easier for people to introduce themselves to me. I usually don't get that. I think that when you see someone at a party, and they are uncomfortable with themselves, that is the last person you want to go over to.

Laura: In situations like this I usually have a great time until I have to tell these people I am an actor. I am really comfortable in social situations with people who are in the business when it is in a social setting; not in their office. That always changes the moment they say, "What do you do?" I feel embarrassed to tell them.

Book: That is part of what this exercise was about. As that moment came up for you in the exercise, did you focus on witnessing it?

Laura: Yes.

Book: How did it go for you?

Laura: It went well. I had a moment of recognition with, "Oh, here is that dreaded moment." But then I inwardly laughed at myself and went right back into the witness and stayed being myself.

Book: She has described a situation that comes up frequently in the social life of actors, where it is a part of your job to take advantage of networking and opportunities to advance your career. Whenever an opportunity presents itself to Laura, inevitably there comes a time when she has to reveal that she is an actor. She always has a negative response to that moment. She is embarrassed because she feels something is at stake and puts herself down for being in that needy position. Here, when she was a witness, that negativity disappeared. Her witness allowed her to discover that she could be amused at her plight, revealing she's an actor, instead of being a victim. So you have Laura, in this case, experientially discovering a major tool along with an exact moment to employ that tool in the future. The witness allows you to shift your perspective, to stand outside the action in a restful place. Shifting your perspective takes the fear and resentment away because you are in the moment, not dwelling in the past and not anticipating the future.

When you were playing the power person, did you notice anything about your partner that seemed different? Typical answers include: The actors were wittier; They had more presence and were ballsy; They seemed much more relaxed and confident; The energy was heightened; It felt just like people talking to people; It was just being in a conversation without the equivalent of the power moment or any sales pitches.

Using your witness provokes more authenticity while being more social. Being in the witness allows you to diminish your losses. There is less self-judgment. Witness mode allows you greater self-awareness about when you act as a victim and it gives you the power to change that to your advantage. Using your witness makes you equal to those who have the power to help your career. When you feel equal, you feel powerful.

General Interview Exercise #6

We will now apply the witness in an interview situation. If you cannot do this exercise with a friend, read through the exercise. You will benefit more from actually participating in the exercise, but will still benefit from reading through it. You may also practice it the next time you have an actual interview. In this round of casting director interviews, your focus will be to *do the interview as a witness*. The interviewer is the casting director at one of the larger studios that produces many TV series—Paramount, let's say. She is having general meetings with actors she hasn't met.

Prior to entering the interview, do your witness preparation process. You might start by rekindling the experience of moving your arms before you get to the walking. Do the arms first, focusing on stop-and-go still pictures of the movement and then changing to fluid movement while keeping your focus on where the stop moments had been. Eventually you should have a feeling of separation. Then when you really feel that, start to walk and immediately apply the feeling to the walk. Heighten it as you walk so you can feel the separation. Now look around and see all the objects in the room or hallway. When you think you are done and you are in your witness mode, then say to yourself, "Can I be more on top of my body? Can I really separate and see what is going on?" Then go in for the interview. Open the door as a witness. See the casting director from above. Sit down and conduct the interview from your witness mode. Throughout the interview you will continually be able to see for the first time: the interviewer, yourself, the two of you together, and the progress of the meeting. Should you find that you are off your witness focus in the interview, find a gesture that you can observe—perhaps you can take a handkerchief from your pocket and clean your glasses or raise your arm from the side of the chair and scratch your forehead. Coach yourself to watch the gesture from your witness, which is similar to raising and lowering your arms. Take charge of your self-coaching and redirect your focus back to watching the interview from above.

In addition, witness yourself employing and practicing all the interview tools that you have learned.

Workshop Actors' Interviews

General Interview Exercise #6—Josh

Josh: Hello.

Casting Director: Hello, Josh. How are you?

Josh: Fine. How are you?

Casting Director: Fine.

Josh: That's a cell phone.

Casting Director: A very big cell phone.

Josh: It's not very compact. You got a Palm Pilot? Is that what that is?

Casting Director: Yeah. It's like a, uh—

Josh: Or are you beaming yourself up?

Casting Director: This isn't actually mine, but I think it's like a phone and a Palm Pilot and like, uh—

Josh: And a television . . .

Casting Director: I think it does everything.

Josh: You know, nowadays, what can't you do with those things?

Casting Director: I know.

Josh: I'm waiting for one to have a little makeup artist in it, so you go (*Makes a sound*) and it just makes you up before you go onstage.

Casting Director: Oh look, it does work like a mirror, too.

Josh: See, that's the beginning of it. That's the beginning of the makeup. Wouldn't that be awesome?

Casting Director: This would be awesome. Even regular women's makeup. I can't tell you how many times I didn't feel like putting on my makeup. Wouldn't it be something? . . . just look at it and bingo!

Josh: (*Laughing*) Yes! And there would be so many things we could do with that. I mean, you could actually have some little guy just pop out and tell you you're wonderful all day long.

Casting Director: That'd be cool.

Josh: The perfect thought.

Casting Director: What about somebody who'd do all your work for you?

Josh: Now we're talking.

Casting Director: Something to clean the house. I want something to clean the house, do the laundry, and . . .

Josh: Now we're talking cloning.

Casting Director: Yeah. That's weird, though.

Josh: You think it's weird?

Casting Director: I think it's weird.

Josh: I think it'd be weird if the clone looked better than we did.

Casting Director: (*Laughing*)

Josh: I think that would be all wrong.

Casting Director: If it was sexier and, like, cuter . . .

Josh: And had better moves.

Casting Director: Yeah. Now they're actually talking about cloning animals that people would eat: the meat and the milk.

Josh: Really!

Casting Director: And I just think that's gross.

Josh: Well, I do, too, because I'm a vegetarian. So I say clone the animals so we can have more petting zoos. Wouldn't that be awesome? All the kids could go and they get to pet the animals. But the clones are cleaner. No diseases. No hoof-and-mouth. (*Picks up the phone and waves it*) Now we need a doctor to pop out. I think one invention is going to lead to the next. (*Both are laughing*) We'd have such a great business. We should be partners.

Casting Director: We should do it. We should. All right.

Josh: Yes! And I have my cell phone.

Casting Director: You do?

Josh: Yeah, we all . . . Oh! Maybe my cell phone wants to meet your cell phone! (*Big laugh as Josh takes out his own cell phone with his other hand*) Let's check it out, okay?

Casting Director: They might already be friends.

Josh: (*Talking to his cell phone*) Hey. Come on, little guy.

Casting Director: Is he shy?

Josh: (*Doing a hand ballet with both phones*) Come on, little guy.
You don't want to come . . .? Come on. Come on, little guy. Aw
. . . He's just kind of . . . Aw, come on! Come on, little guy.

Casting Director: The camera scared him off.

Josh: It's just a camera. It's just a camera.

Casting Director: He's just shy. Don't worry.

Josh: Aw . . .

Casting Director: He's so cute.

Josh: (*His hands are now holding the phones so they are rubbing
against each other.*) Oh! Oh! What is that? What are you
doing?

Casting Director: (*Laughing*) Look, he's showing off. That is
so cute!

Josh: Whoa. Whoa! Phone sex! Phone sex! Oh. Bad phone.
Bad phone.

Casting Director: Well, I don't know.

Josh: You know ringtones? You can buy a song for like ninety-
nine cents, but a ringtone's like two ninety-nine.

Casting Director: What's a ringtone?

Josh: A ringtone's like, uh . . . uh . . .

Casting Director: Is it different from having a song?

Josh: I'll show you. It's like having a . . . but it's a portion . . .
(*He plays a ringtone on his phone and sings along with it while
dancing a few steps.*) "Lips like sugar . . ." I paid like two
ninety-nine for that.

Casting Director: That one song?

Josh: Just that. It plays over and over. But I can pay ninety-
nine cents for the whole song. (*He plays another ringtone:
Wham's "Careless Whisper"*)

Casting Director: (*Cracking up*) Is that George Michael?

Josh: (*Whistles a few bars*) Okay, that's enough of that.

Casting Director: That's great.

Josh: (*To his phone*) You did good, you little boy! Well, it was very nice meeting you.

Casting Director: It was a pleasure, Josh. I'll remember you.

General Interview Exercise #6 — Lisa

Lisa: Hi. How are you?

Casting Director: Good. How are you?

Lisa: Good.

Casting Director: Nice to meet you.

Lisa: Nice to meet you. You have a green band.

Casting Director: I do.

Lisa: A bracelet. (*Her speech rhythm picks up speed*) You ever wish you didn't say something because once it's out of your mouth you realize it might be the stupidest thing anyone's said ever? Like if I'd said, "Oh, there's a table!" and you'd say, "I know there's a table. There's clearly a table because I'm sitting at the table, it's probably been here for years," and you know you have a bracelet because you're wearing the bracelet and your kid probably gave it to you, which is really nice, to have kids who love you and give you stuff, because I don't think I've given my parents anything for a while—Well, unless you count the parking ticket that I gave my dad to pay for me, because—Well, he had taken my car to borrow it, and it was really dirty, so—He borrowed it because he has a really small car and he needed it to take people to the airport. So I had gone down to his house to see his new dog, which is named Go-Away, because he doesn't like dogs. So I went to go see Go-Away, and my dad took my car to go take his business partner to the airport, and while he was gone, he noticed two things: one, the car was despicably dirty, and two, there was a parking ticket right on top of the dashboard, which, to be honest, I happened to leave there on purpose, because it was inside the glove compartment, but I thought, "Dad's taking my car—I'll leave the parking ticket out, throw away cigarette boxes" . . . Not that I would ever smoke, because I know smoking is bad for your health.

Casting Director: Of course.

Lisa: That's not the point. The point is, Dad sees the parking ticket, he thinks: "Oh, Lisa, she's such a flake. I'd best pay the parking ticket, right after I wash her car," because honestly he's right—cars look better after they're cleaned, even though my car . . . (*Pause*) No, my car died on Wednesday. It was killed, honestly in a wreck.

Casting Director: Oh, dear.

Lisa: But before that, it was the color of dirt. Now it's the color of dirt, only it's smaller. In front. It's the same size in the back, only it's a little scratched up, and I don't think that anyone wants the back of a car for anything, especially if the car can't go anywhere, which my car can't, because the radiator is almost inside the passenger seat, which would be cute, except that's where my dog likes to sit.

Casting Director: Were you—

Lisa: Point being, sometimes really stupid things come out of my mouth, and then you have to think to yourself, "This poor girl has the dumbest—" (*Pause*) "Has the dumbest stuff," I can censor, "coming out of her mouth, which is too bad because she could be a nice, cute girl if it weren't for the ridiculously bright pink bra strap coming out of her shirt, which kind of actually matches the fact that she's wearing too much blush and not enough lipstick." Point being (*Pause, taps her teeth with her nails*)

Casting Director: I don't agree.

Lisa: If I tap on my on teeth, I might get a thought.

Casting Director: I can hear that over here. You're doing it very loud.

Lisa: (*Having stopped tapping, she moves her finger to the air around her ear and makes circles.*) I can still hear it right here.

Casting Director: Really?

Lisa: Kind of.

Casting Director: Is it like a song in your head?

Lisa: No, but it hurts.

Casting Director: Oh.

Lisa: A little.

Casting Director: I'm sorry. I hope you weren't—

Lisa: Now I'm embarrassed.

Casting Director: I hope you weren't in your car when it got wrecked.

Lisa: (*Delighted*) Oh, I was! I was driving it. I drove it right into the person right in front of me, which is a bummer, 'cause it would've been my fault—Well, it is my fault. It's always your fault when you drive into the person in front of you. I remember that, but luckily for me, the person behind me also drove into me, re-driving me into the person in front of me, and thereby helping me share the blame, which I don't think, honestly, is going to stop my insurance from dropping me, I'll be honest, because (*Squeaks*) this is my fifth wreck in three or four—How long have I lived here? I've been living here a long time.

Casting Director: Have you?

Lisa: I have lived here since (*Pause*) December of two—(*Gasps*)

Casting Director: December of 2000? That's actually not that long.

Lisa: Thank you.

Casting Director: That's only five years.

Lisa: It's like a college education without any schooling.

Casting Director: Yes. I've heard L.A. can be described that way.

Lisa: And it's sunny, which is nice, which is how I got my really nice tan.

Casting Director: Yes, you're very tan. I can see that. Just looking at you, how tan you are.

Lisa: Yeah, so, there's a bunch of pencils in there. (*Gesturing to a pencilholder*)

Casting Director: I know. I obviously use this a lot.

Lisa: Yes! And you can write all sorts of fun things all over my picture after I leave. It's nice meeting you.

Casting Director: Wait. Where are you going?

Lisa: I have to return the rental car or the insurance . . . I have enjoyed meeting you. Bye.

Casting Director: Nice meeting you, too. I have actually enjoyed it a lot.

General Interview Exercise #6 — Anthony

Anthony: Nice to meet you.

Casting Director: You, too.

Anthony: That's a Starbucks coffee cup.

Casting Director: Yes. A venti.

Anthony: I hate that. We don't live in Italy. This is America. There's three sizes: small, medium, and large. And given the expanding size of most Americans, we've changed them to extra-large, husky, and on-the-verge-of-a-heart-attack.

Casting Director: (*Laughing*). You from L.A.?

Anthony: I am from Quantico, Virginia, specifically, FBI headquarters, third floor, special division: casting surveillance. (*Pointing to plant*) You think this is an ordinary ficus. It's actually a listening device. We are monitoring your activities. The government wants to put a stop to miscasting in feature films: George Clooney as Batman, Cedric the Entertainer as Ralph Kramden, and anything with Pauly Shore or Tom Arnold in it.

Casting Director: (*Laughs*)

Anthony: Yes! And that's why we are here. We'd like to talk to you about that.

Casting Director: We?

Anthony: My partner and I.

Casting Director: He's out in your car?

Anthony: He's actually right here. (*Points to backpack*)

Casting Director: How're you doing?

Anthony: (*Reaches into backpack and takes out a space figure, changes voice to play a character*) I'm Special Agent Orange. Have you seen any reality-TV producers lurking in the building? We understand they have been operating in this area pitching new shows.

Casting Director: Not in this office they haven't!

Anthony: No one's approached you to cast *I Want To Be a Circus Freak*?

Casting Director: No.

Anthony: You haven't seen any women with beards?

Casting Director: No.

Anthony: No dog-faced children?

Casting Director: No.

Anthony: No Republicans with a heart and an eye for social programs?

Casting Director: (*Laughs*)

Anthony: This is not a laughing matter, woman! (*As Anthony*) Orange! Orange! Calm down. Let me handle this. As you can see my partner is very passionate about this. His mother used to be shot out of a cannon. (*As Agent Orange*) I know her type! "We'll get ice cream as soon as Mommy's done with work." Next thing you know: There's a big bang, Mommy has a headache, no ice cream for little Billy Orange. (*As Anthony*) Why don't you go back in the bag and let me handle this? (*He opens backpack and watches the space figure get into it.*) I'm terribly sorry about that.

Casting Director: I've had a troubled childhood, too.

Anthony: Yes! And I think it's time you talk about it.

Casting Director: Oh, I don't think so.

Anthony: Then the healing can't start. But that's a personal decision. Just so you know, I'm here when you're ready. I know how difficult it can be to confront your personal demons. (*He waves invisible demons away from his body*) I, too, have come to a crossroads in my life. Due to my slight myopia I can never be a fighter pilot. (*Sadly*) Oh, how I've dreamed of sitting in that cockpit on the flight deck as the engines rattle beneath me. (*His faux sadness builds intensity throughout following*) I begin to roll down the tarmac faster and faster as I ease the stick back. I feel the surge of freedom rise in my loins, growing stronger and stronger until lift off, piercing through the clouds singly focused on my mission— (*Almost weeping*) fighting for God, Country, and Kelly McGillis. (*He bursts into song*)

Watching every motion in my foolish lover's game
On this endless ocean finally lovers know no shame
Turning and returning to some secret place inside
Watching in slow motion as you turn around and say
Take my breath away
Take my breath away . . .

Casting Director: (*Laughing throughout*) That's very good. You sing, too.

Anthony: Yes. The only song I can't sing is "I Can See Clearly Now" by Johnnie Nash. (*His voice changes to a muffled Agent Orange voice, singing*) I can see clearly now the rain is gone. (*Back to Anthony's voice, talking to backpack*) Shut up. You're embarrassing me. (*Orange's voice*) I can see all obstacles in my way. (*Anthony's voice, to Casting Director*) I'm terribly sorry. We have to go. (*Talking to backpack*) How many times do I have to tell you not to do that when we're with people? (*Orange's voice*) Gonna be bright, bright . . . She likes me better! . . . Bright, sun-shiny day.

Casting Director: (*Laughing*) Bye.

General Interview Exercise #6 — Shannon

Shannon: Well hello.

Casting Director: Hi.

Shannon: Shannon. Nice to meet you.

Casting Director: Nice to meet you. Have a seat.

Shannon: Thank you. Oh my gosh, that's a huge tree!

Casting Director: Yeah.

Shannon: I love trees. And your office can really support a tree. Ordinarily, you don't have enough light.

Casting Director: We've got light here.

Shannon: Yeah, there's tons of windows. You know also, plants inside, they help you think clearer, and be more alert, because they're cleansing the air all the time.

Casting Director: They're cleansing the air all the time?

Shannon: Yes, they are. You didn't know that? It takes out—I know they give off carbon—No, they take in carbon dioxide. They give off oxygen.

Casting Director: So I've got a little oxygen plant off in the corner?

Shannon: Yes. You have your own little air purifier over there. There's actually certain plants that are supposed to take out certain toxins. There's actually one that's called—(*Gestures the shape of a large plant*) Mother-in-law's tongue. Have you seen that one?

Casting Director: Yes.

Shannon: That's right. I see. You're married.

Casting Director: (*Laughs*)

Shannon: Yes, but, these long green kind of sword things, and supposedly, if you get a new carpet—There's a lot of chemicals in the carpet, and if you don't want to smell that—

Casting Director: That Dacron smell or whatever?

Shannon: Yeah. However, if you have a good carpet layer, they roll out the carpet outside, and they leave it outside for a while—I hope it's not raining. They leave it outside for a while, and a lot of that stuff airs out before it comes into your house.

Casting Director: Well, that's a good thing.

Shannon: Yeah, so that way you don't get all that stuff. But if you do, get that sword plant—

Casting Director: Mother-in-law's tongue?

Shannon: That's what it's called. Someday I'll be a mother-in-law, so I don't want to make that stereotype go any further.

Casting Director: Well, you could be the one to turn it around for all the mothers-in-law out there.

Shannon: Thank you. I hope so. I've got a while. My kids are very young, so I've got a while before—

Casting Director: Boys or girls?

Shannon: Girls.

Casting Director: Really?

Shannon: Two girls.

Casting Director: Two girls?

Shannon: Yes.

Casting Director: I have two girls, too.

Shannon: Do you? Oh, they're wonderful. I love that—How old are your girls?

Casting Director: Four and six weeks.

Shannon: Oh my gosh! So why are you awake?

Casting Director: Because there's nothing else to do. I can't be asleep.

Shannon: When my kids were six weeks, I was asleep constantly.

Casting Director: Really?

Shannon: I'd be like, putting dinner, and all of a sudden . . . (*Drops her head and snores*)

Casting Director: Well that's got to—

Shannon: Like one time, I was making the bed. And it just looked so nice. And I just put my head on it while I was standing, and I completely fell asleep standing there. (*Laughs*)

Casting Director: (*Laughing*) With your head—

Shannon: With my head on the bed. And it just felt so good (*Laughs*). And my husband walked by. He's like: "Honey? Are you all right?" And I went: "Huh? What?" But I really wish that he'd just let me sleep, because it felt so wonderful to just lay there. But I thought, "Man, that's really sad, to just fall asleep standing up," because I thought, "What am I? A horse?" (*Laughs*)

Casting Director: (*Laughing*) Yep!

Shannon: (*Laughs*) Oh my gosh! But, yeah—I'm really surprised that you're so awake.

Casting Director: I'm the lucky one. My husband lets me sleep through the night. But my daughter's starting to sleep like six or seven hours a night.

Shannon: Wow! At six weeks? Oh, that's tremendous.

Casting Director: Yeah, but like from nine to four in the morning, so I'm still up at the crack of dawn.

Shannon: I know. There's something about children. You want to—I know. I would never do this. Really. But you kind of want to have sort of like an alarm clock or something that when they get out of bed it would knock them on the head or something so they fall back asleep.

Casting Director: (*Laughs*)

Shannon: Because my kids are older—

Casting Director: Oh God, if I told anybody that, they'd lock you away.

Shannon: I know. If anyone's listening, I really don't mean that.

Casting Director: But if it's just me, right?

Shannon: My kids are seven and five and I swear to God, during the school year, because my daughter's in first grade, she is up, dragged out of bed. She will not get out of bed.

Six-thirty in the morning, you have to drag her out of bed. Weekends, she's up at five.

Casting Director: Oh God.

Shannon: And it's not like we let them go and watch cartoons or eat sugary cereal or anything like that. So basically she hasn't got anything to do except wake us up. And that's very important to her.

Casting Director: So in she comes.

Shannon: So in she comes, right. So I don't know why it is. She tells time. How does she know—? I guess she knows it's the weekend because there's no school. But it's like an internal clock thing.

Casting Director: I know.

Shannon: You keep them up late and it doesn't matter.

Casting Director: I'm looking forward to school. My four-year-old gets up at five A.M. anyway—

Shannon: Really?

Casting Director: Comes in and just stands there next to the clock until it's six.

Shannon: Right. "You told me to wait until it says six, zero, zero."

Casting Director: "Mommy, I'm waiting until it says six."

Shannon: Wait in your room, will you? Come on, kid. Get out of here (*Laughs*). And it's just amazing. And also, they're so darn quiet. At least my kids are.

Casting Director: They're quiet?

Shannon: No, not in that way. She sneaks into the room and you don't know that she's there. And she's standing right there by the bed, and she's standing just like this. (*Holds her hand right over her face*) And you have this feeling, lying there, thinking, "What's going on?" And then you suddenly open your eyes, and there's this face, standing there.

Casting Director: (*Laughs*).

Shannon: And of course you go: "Aaaahhh!" And then I wake up my husband. So then he's not so happy with me. So I tell her, "You know, if you want to wake up Momma, just come and touch me real light, and that would be great."

Casting Director: Right, but this standing over me and making me paranoid, not so good.

Shannon: Right. Don't just stand there. 'Cause I've found that I'm jarred awake at like three in the morning, thinking she's standing there over me.

Casting Director: (*Laughs*) You're having like flashbacks.

Shannon: I am. See, I never saw *Psycho*. But I'm hoping one day I don't have this flashback of her standing there over me with a knife or something. 'Cause I mean, it's just creepy!

Casting Director: Try to get on her good side.

Shannon: Well, you try to do that anyway. You'll find out as they get older. You just try to stay on their good side as much as you can.

Casting Director: (*Laughs*)

Shannon: Really. This is my advice to you.

Casting Director: Really?

Shannon: Please take it. I've experienced this.

Casting Director: Really? Just cave?

Shannon: Every time.

Casting Director: That's the secret to happy parenting?

Shannon: Happy daughters, happy parents.

Casting Director: Peace at any price.

Shannon: I tell you. That's it. I've just fixed your life. Look at that. Well, it's been a pleasure.

Casting Director: Quite so. Thank you very much.

Shannon: Have a good day.

Casting Director: Come again.

Follow-Up Questions

After doing the exercise ask yourself the following questions:

Were you able to stay on focus?

Did you arrive at the interview in your witness mode?

Did you conduct a good part of the interview in witness mode?

Do you think you had a sense of payoff from the witness?

Keeping in mind how the actors we are tracking began this interview project, did you notice that there was no victim behavior anymore? The interviewer could sit back and enjoy herself. She never had the feeling that she had to take care of anybody. There were quite a few interviews in which she didn't even have to say a word. She never felt manipulated or felt as if she had to deal with any dishonesty. When you do interviews like this, you will stand out from the other actors.

> **Shannon:** It seemed very obvious that there was always more to do. Like, I didn't have to look for it. If anything, I had to pick only one thing to do when there were so clearly fifty of them, as opposed to before, being: "Uh, you have a chair." This time, it was: "You have a chair, and a table, and a cup, and hair, and a plant, and I'm wearing shoes."

> **Anthony:** The thing I really hit on in this interview was, I think, that I wanted to explore or intensify whatever emotions came up for me, and I wanted to take them further than I ordinarily would've. So I got a little angry about something, I

got damn angry about it! And I got big with it. I got sad, I got big with it. I just wanted to get big with everything, and I think the witness mode allowed me to do that.

Josh: I felt—I saw where I was, and I could make a decision about where I wanted to go, and coach myself to get there, rather than merely... When I'm not in the witness mode, sometimes I'll just be passingly aware of what state I'm in and not in control of it at the same time. And the witness mode allows me to be both cognizant of it, and in control of it. And that's great.

Lisa: The witness really affected my extending and intensifying. Last time, I felt as if I was putting on a show. And this time it felt very integrated with what I was saying, very natural. It just went. Being in the witness allowed me to see so many opportunities for funny moments. I felt like I was getting laughs without any effort. So that was a lot of fun and a very—a good payoff. So many of these interviews were funny. *How important is it to be funny in an interview?*

Book: If you *happen to be funny* as a part of creating an experience, that will make the experience more enjoyable for the interviewer. If you *try to be funny*, that will work against you and trigger your victim stance and manipulation.

Tracy: I wasn't nervous. There were moments of nervousness but there wasn't the, "Oh my God, what am I going to say when I get in there?" It was just much more enjoyable. I wasn't going through the, "Oh my God, what if I don't find anything to tell a truth about?" It was easy to see and tell a truth. I just had a trust that there was going to be something to talk about.

Book: An important part of the witness-preparation process is taking a ride on your own body and seeing the sights around you. One of those sights can be what you tell your truth about.

You are increasing the potential of available truths to talk about because you more readily see them.

Larry: There was this moment of silence, and I got into this slightly panicky mode of being on my own and I saw myself—from up on top—judging instead of witnessing. When I saw that, I just said to myself, "No. Don't go there." Then the witness superseded the judge and moved me forward. That made it okay for the next subject to just reveal itself to me and I went with it.

James: When the Casting Director looked down at my résumé, I knew I was in trouble. However, I realized at that moment that I really was in my witness place. Instead of getting all frazzled, I was kind of up there and I giggled at myself. It was just great.

Book: That is the experience. That is one of the biggest benefits of doing this from your witness. If something goes slightly wrong or slightly ajar, or you say something slightly silly, you are witness to it and you see it for just what it is, just a moment of slight silliness, or slight incorrectness, or a slight mishap. You don't, as a victim, go into an overbearing response that is way too much for the event. It is the difference between saying to yourself, "I made a little mistake" rather than, "Oh my God, I am so damn stupid. What did I just do?" With the latter, you then blow the entire rest of the interview, suffering from your mistake. You throw the rest of your good time away for the little tiny mistake.

James: You have to be able to let it go. We are all human beings.

Book: That is why you are a witness and not a judge.

Andrew: It makes failure much more enjoyable. When we did the interview for the first time, and I really failed, I walked out of class and I was really beating myself up.

This time, I walked away with, "Okay, I'll get it next time. Whatever."

Laura: Watching people's victim stuff from before, and this time how, what they did with their victim stuff. Like, the way all of a sudden someone who laughs when it's not funny is laughing until it becomes funny. Like some of the things that people do were there, but this time they were using them and benefiting from them as opposed to being a victim of them.

Linda: I interviewed Shannon, and I had a great experience with her. I just felt like she took me down this walk where we were just laughing, having this incredible time together. I thought she was really natural and she was just talking to me as a person. She wasn't doing a bit. She wasn't manipulating. She was just fun. I couldn't believe it was over when she walked out of there. I wanted to just reach out and bring her back in.

Summary

Adding your witness to your interview technique makes interviewing easier. The interview itself becomes almost effortless. Your witness allows you to see more clearly what is, rather than what you *think* is. When interviewers have attitudes, i.e., acting impatient or disrespectful, you might think they don't like you. But the witness allows you to see that it is not about you, it is about them, and that realization will stop you from becoming a victim. The witness allows you to get past their negative behavior and employ your other interview tools. When you do that, guess what happens? The interviewers' behavior changes, and they begin enjoying themselves. You will be the one they will notice, remember, and want to see again.

It is very powerful to do an interview with your witness turned on. You never become flustered, manipulative, or a victim because you are up on top seeing everything for what it is rather than what you think it is. Being in the moment and simultaneously witnessing it allow you to select spontaneously and effortlessly any appropriate tools, e.g., Enlarge, Extend, and Intensify; tell another truth; Reflection Listening; Yes! And . . . This translates into still more confidence, which will heighten your desire and ability to stay even more on focus.

The Waiting-Room Witness

Here is an easy and somewhat anonymous preparation for utilizing your witness prior to your interviews or auditions. With adjustments you can do it in a waiting room without anyone's being aware.

Setup

Sit in a chair, either in an actual waiting room or in a space that simulates a waiting room, with your usual assortment of accessories, e.g., your purse, backpack, newspaper, appointment book, portfolio, etcetera. For five minutes, you will either simulate or actually wait to go into an interview.

Acting Focus

The witness.

Waiting-Room Witness Exercise

Observe your breathing. Focus on your breathing. Raise your arm as high as your shoulder in a *series of still pictures*. Move it a little, stop, move it a little, stop. Then lower it the same way. As you do this, focus on the feeling of being the witness, which, as you remember, is similar to doing nothing. Raise your arm as a witness, and lower your arm as a witness. Maintain the same focus and allow your arm to move up and down in *normal speed* without stopping. Maintain the same focus, but now move it in *triple speed*, still focusing on the witness. Now return to *normal speed*. Since you're doing nothing, you are free to observe your arm as if it has nothing to do with you. You are now focusing on being the witness. Reach for an accessory, a prop, but stay out of it. You merely observe your body as it reaches and finds different things. It's your body that's busy, not you. If you are using space objects, allow your body to respect the space objects that it handles while you stay out of it.

Continue to allow your body to find and use objects while you do nothing, but now extend your vision out so you are enjoying the sights in the waiting room. You're free to watch anybody else in the room. This is the feeling of the witness. Remain here for one minute—one minute to allow your body to do whatever it wants while you stay out of it and witness the other people. Add another sight—yourself doing the activity. You're not involved in the doing of any activity; that's your body's job. But you're sitting on top of your body enjoying watching yourself do the activity.

When the receptionist calls your name to go in, stay in the witness as you say thank-you, put away any objects, and begin walking across the room. Take a ride on your own body. Focus on the witness while you walk. Do not look for something magical to happen; if you're looking for something to happen, you'll get in your own way. With each step you take, see all the new sights. You're doing nothing, and since you're doing nothing, you have the time and opportunity to view everything. Enter the interviewer's office.

Follow-Up Questions

Are you finding it easier to get into the witness?

Are you increasing this feeling of doing nothing?

Are you extending the amount of time you can take a ride on your own body?

Are you coaching yourself to stay on focus?

Summary

The waiting room can be a dangerous place for the actor because there are many potential distractions to keep you from being in a focused and relaxed state. If you should become distracted then you will go into the meeting or audition tense, which is sure to trigger inauthenticity and your victim stance.

The waiting room is full of surprises, most of them potentially disastrous for you. For example, let's say you spent fifteen dollars for the sides from a casting website at a dollar a page, but the casting assistant informs that you will only be reading the first three pages. You will have an emotional reaction to having spent the extra twelve dollars while you should be focusing on your work. Or how about those thin walls between the waiting room and the audition room? While you are focusing on preparing or relaxing, you hear all of the other actors before you. You can't help but listen. Now you are confronted with a decision: Do you stay with what you prepared or do you change it so it jives with what they wanted from the other actors? By now, you are no longer focused. Also, how about the other actors in the waiting room? They contribute to the potential danger, too. Some of them are acting out their inauthenticities: the victim who is so scared that he keeps spilling his coffee and apologizing profusely to everyone; the manipulator who only wants to engage you in conversation about how many auditions and meetings she has had that day; the drama queen who is carrying on with the casting assistant over a time change.

If you are in the witness mode during this time, you will see everything for what it is in a detached manner. Just because there are distractions, you don't have to get hooked into them. Feel empowered by your ability to avoid entering the fray. This will heighten your confidence and turn a negative into a positive.

The "I Am" Witness

One more use for the witness is to help you take on the attitude line of "I am." After you learn how to do it, you can practice this focus to increase the amount of time that you're capable of sustaining the witness and your attitude of "I am."

Setup

Coach yourself to retain the attitude line "I am" from Chapter 5, then start walking around the room.

Rules and Acting Focus

Walk around, holding the attitude line of "I am." Now while you're walking, go into the witness. You're watching with a pair of eyes three inches above your head. See through those eyes. You don't have to be absolutely literal—get the sense of seeing from above you. Your body feels elongated. Now, while you're up there, you can move your arm up and down, fluidly, and see it from the witness. As you make gestures in the space, retain "I am," and see your arm from above you. Get a feeling that it's not your own arm, but someone else's arm. It does what it wants. You're not involved. Now put your arm down and walk—take a ride on your own body. Bring your "I am" into the witness.

Follow-Up Question

Were you able to have some success with retaining your "I am" with the witness?

Summary

You can choose, while you're waiting for your next interview, to take on the "I am" attitude and get into the witness.

9

It's Your Career

Three-Phone-Calls-a-Day Exercise

If you would like to increase your number of career interviews and opportunities, introduce this exercise into your daily life. Instead of sitting and waiting for the phone to ring—which is a victim stance—make three business phone calls a day, Monday through Friday. Do this and your career will improve greatly. Treat it like a game in which you will have to figure out whom to call and what to say. If acting is doing and there's always more to do, then career is doing and there's always more to do. Of course you must continue with everything you are already doing to advance your career, i.e., sending out pictures and résumés, following up on agent and manager leads, going to open calls, attending an experiential class in which you work in every class. Starting today—or tomorrow at the latest—make three extra phone calls a day for business.

The game aspect of this exercise is coming up with the daily list of three contacts. You might try a call to an agent whom a friend talked about. Perhaps you could call a theater director you met at a party. This exercise will force you to be creative and diligent in extending your career. If you do the exercise for just one week, you will have created energy in fifteen new areas. After a year, 480! Put that much more energy out there and you will see a return on your investment.

Compare this approach to that of someone who only sends pictures and résumés to the opportunities he or she sees in *Back Stage* and then waits for the phone to ring. Three phone calls a day is not outrageous. If you take on this challenge, you will create many more opportunities for yourself. By the time you have made fifty new calls, one of them may lead to something. And while you are pursuing these calls you will, at least, feel much better about yourself and your career because you are being proactive instead of feeling helpless, which enhances your victim stance.

You would be cheating yourself if you substitute e-mail for telephone calls. E-mail is too easily sent and too easily deleted. However, the Internet and your computer may be great resource tools for finding whom to call and keeping track of your calls.

Rick Pagano—a casting director for film, TV, and theater—advises, "If I were an actor, I would call all the casting directors who are in the book. Ten of them may get angry. The ones who pick up the phones and talk to you are the ones you want to do business with anyway. You'd be amazed at how many people actually do take your phone calls, and how many people do want your picture and résumé. Think of yourself as a salesman. They go and knock at a hundred doors and ninety-five will say no, but five might say yes. Most of the time, when you call a casting office, you might end up talking with an assistant. But remember, in this business, this year's assistant is maybe next year's casting director. Be your own cheerleader, your own inspirer, and your own secretary. Call people and try to meet every agent and casting director. If we the casting community don't know you exist, how are we going to hire you? Do take charge of your career. Don't be a victim. We need your uniqueness.[1]

Photo Sessions

You will find that the Attitude Line acting focus is an excellent tool for photo shoots for your commercial or theatrical photos. Pick from, or alternate between:

Women

Do you want that sexy, vixenish look?
"I love men,"
"I am sensual,"
"I'm a flirt."

Do you want that professional white-collar look? Try:
"I have integrity,"
"I'm in control."

A powerful and bad woman? Try:
"I want it all,"
"I can do this."

The good mom? Try:
"I'm in charge,"
"I care."

Men

Do you want that goofy friend look? Try:
"I'm enthusiastic."

How about a bad guy? Try:
"I'm mean."

The good father? Try:
"I'm decent,"
"I know it all."

A blue-collar tough guy? Try:
"I'm the boss!"

A white-collar professional? Try:
"I have integrity,"
"I'm in charge,"
"I'm confident."

Charming leading man? Try:
"I'm easy,"
"I have to."

The Professional Actor is a Business Person

Always remember that show business is a business. Casting directors, agents, directors, and producers respect actors who present themselves in a business-like way. You should not be late for appointments. You never present excuses. For auditions, you have done your work and are prepared. Your materials are in order, such as . . .

Pictures and Résumés

When you submit your picture and résumé, make sure they are stapled together. Delivering unattached pictures and résumés communicates that you are either a complete novice or passive-aggressive. You communicate that you resent having to submit your picture and résumé to anyone (victim stance). If you bring an unattached picture and résumé to an interview or audition, you are setting yourself up for inauthenticity because the interviewer will start the meeting with a comment such as, "You should staple your picture to the résumé." Your response will always make you look foolish, and your meeting will be off to a terrible start.

Here are two examples of these kinds of exchanges:

Casting Director: You should staple your picture to the résumé.

Actor: Oh, I'm sorry. I just picked them up from the printer and didn't have time to staple them.

This sends the message to the casting director that you are a liar because you could have stapled one or two at the printer. This excuse is a cover-up for passive-aggressive communication.

Casting Director: Why don't you staple these together? They get separated and we don't know whose picture goes with which résumé.

Actor: Well, my name is on the picture so you can figure it out.

The casting director now hates you because you are being defensive and telling him that it's okay if he does the additional work of matching up the separated pictures and résumés.

The appropriate response that will not exacerbate a situation is, "Thanks for the tip. This is my first professional meeting." And if it isn't, why are you still handing out unattached pictures and résumés?

Monologues

It is a wise actor who always has a prepared and polished monologue or two. An interviewer may offer you the opportunity to do a monologue, and it would be a shame not to be in a position to take advantage of this opportunity. I have always respected an actor who suggests that he or she does a monologue for me. I usually take them up on it. Offering to do a monologue is another way of turning an interview into an audition.

Office Behavior

Never be rude or obnoxious to office assistants. They will tell their bosses, and the casting director will never risk sending a badly behaved actor to a set. Badly behaved actors reflect poorly on the casting director. Also, remember that the receptionist you are rude to today may be tomorrow's casting director. Your bad behavior will be remembered.

After the Interview

Actors who truly understand that the pursuit of their career is a business adopt a system of keeping records, usually a card file or a contacts journal. After any interview or audition, follow up by writing down all the specifics: date of the meeting; whom you met with; what the results were; anything you did or spoke about that enhanced the meeting or limited it; your own assessment of the meeting. With auditions, you should add: name of the project; what part you read for; who eventually got the part; what you think you did or did not do to help yourself give the best audition. Write an evaluation of the audition and then profit from your evaluation at the next audition.

The Casting Director/Agent as a Victim or an Intimidator

If your interviewer presents him or herself as a victim, you should definitely not enter into the game by taking care of the individual. Instead, stay grounded and become extremely authentic, tell a truth, and then start enlarging, intensifying, and extending some aspect of your conversation into a heightened experience for both of you. If you can create experiences, you will pull these victims out of their inauthentic victim stances into having authentic experiences with you. They will be thrilled with you for that. Other actors may take care of them, and support them to continue in their victim stances, but they will have been enabled and will be miserable throughout the interview. But if you act as a catalyst to pull them out of their misery, they will have a good time with you, and you will be remembered.

Victim interviewers will usually begin an interview by moaning and groaning about something. Let them do it just long enough to recognize what they are doing. Then say your truth line, which will throw them because no one says a truth to them. They are so used to manipulating people into taking care of them that the truth is the last thing they expect to hear. When someone says a truth to you, they are not taking care of you. They are simply saying what is, which is completely unattached to wanting something, as in, "I will take care of you and in return I want you to give me that audition or represent me."

If your interviewer presents him or herself as an intimidator, you should not become a victim. When you become a victim, you support the other person's continuing to function as an intimidator. When interviewers present themselves as either intimidators or victims, they are reacting to the victim stances of actors. Interviewers are human and get fed up with actors who do not know how to conduct themselves professionally. So if you are relaxed, centered, and totally authentic, they will quickly stop being either victims or intimidators and have an experience with you. They will like and remember you because you will have allowed them to experience a transformation from inauthenticity to authenticity.

Finesse for Success!

How do I request a contact to get me a meeting with someone else?

Make the call and establish rapport without any manipulation or victim stance, i.e., greet the person and briefly chat about something you have in common. Then, as an equal, ask for the favor you want. Don't mess this up by trying to manipulate the conversation so that you get the other person to come up with the idea of, for instance, passing on your picture and résumé to a director. Also, don't drop hints—just ask. Both of these manipulative approaches will not lead to your getting what you want. Make a straightforward request. Don't hedge.

What about lying on my résumé?

Inventing or improving credits is lying up, which is manipulative, inauthentic, and a victim stance manifestation. While in a few cases it might gain you access to an interview or audition, it will always lead to trouble. If you are found out— and you will be—any relationship with the casting director, agent, or manager will be immediately terminated and the door to that office will never be open to you again. Inauthenticity is not the foundation for any relationship. No one likes to feel cheated, and you will have cheated that person. Your picture also should be an accurate representation of you.

Phil Brock, an agent with Studio Talent Group, relates, "One of my character actors, we'll call him Bert, was really right for a beer ad campaign that a commercial CD was casting. This CD issued repeated requests for the type of actor she was looking for, and I repeatedly submitted Bert. But no phone call came. I called the CD and received an earful. She had been an assistant years ago in an MP/TV casting office, and Bert had come in for an audition. It seems Bert had 'upgraded' his role on a Broadway show to the lead, and all hell broke loose in the casting office. The CD blistered Bert for the lie, he wasn't hired, and twenty years later this commercial CD remembered the incident and refused to ever call Bert in for anything, even a commercial. Bert certainly paid for his role upgrade."[2]

Casting director Susan Glicksman adds: "My biggest pet peeve is when an actor comes in with a résumé listing a movie-of-the-week that I know he wasn't in because I cast it!"[3]

Jackie Apodaca writes "The Working Actor" column for *Back Stage West* and says, "Actors need to show prospective employers that they are great performers, but they also need to demonstrate that they are reliable, easygoing, self-assured, sane people. Lies indicate a lack of confidence and a lack of self-possession. They scream, 'I am not really ready for this opportunity!' It's better to proudly embrace what you have than to advertise what you lack."[4]

Lying is a manifestation of being both a victim and a con artist. Additionally, if your agent or manager tells you to pad your résumé with phony credits, you have the wrong person representing you. Casting director Billy DaMota adds, "Every actor starts with a blank résumé. A good manager, agent, or casting director will always take a chance and help develop an actor when they see potential . . . and the résumé grows from there. Patience: It really is a virtue."[5]

How do I handle a telephone or video interview ?

A telephone interview is usually a pre-interview to determine if the interviewer will give you a face-to-face interview. In a telephone interview you will be asked questions about your credits. The interviewer will be judging you on how you handle the telephone meeting, e.g., your attitude. Stay open to answering the questions without becoming a victim or attempting any manipulation—turn your answers into a conversation. Employ your interview tools, especially those of Extend, Intensify, and Enlarge, and guide the conversation away from your credits and into an experience. That experience will be more important than any information you could provide. Despite the obvious limitations of a telephone meeting, you can reveal yourself as authentic and attractive.

Video-conferences are not common, but you may have one after you have been called back. Treat a video-conference as you would a face-to-face interview and use all your interview tools. Be authentic, heighten your presence, and create as much of an experience as you can within the limitations of the situation.

Should I shake hands with the interviewer?

If the interviewer initiates a handshake, then shake hands. You should not initiate a handshake. It starts or ends the meeting with a gesture of you being on your best behavior, a performance. From the interviewer's point of view, he or she doesn't want to grab hands with every one who comes in for a meeting.

Is it better if my first truth line is something substantial rather than a mundane observation?

Some actors get hung up on looking for "a good truth line" rather than a mundane truth line. The longer you evaluate your truth line, the harder it will become to discover this first truth line. *One truth is as good as another.* It is all about where the truth leads, not the subject of the first truth. It is all about the experience that will begin when you say a truth.

What happens if the interviewer's response to my first truth line is a simple agreement?

When you say a truth line, the people you are speaking to might not build upon it. They may simply respond with a simple line like, "Yes, it is." However, that simple line opens

up a channel to receive communication from you, and that
is a strong beginning. Whereas, if the first thing you say to
someone is inauthentic, the exact opposite will happen. People
will shut down. Has anyone tried to pick you up in a bar or
tried to befriend you in any situation with a lot of BS? Your
initial response is to put up a wall. So don't be distraught if all
you get back on your first truth line is, "Yes, it is." You have
created an open channel, at least, and the ball is in your court
to say another truth line. You can't ask for more than that
when you are talking to strangers.

What do I do if interviewers don't shut up?

If that happens, you have an opportunity to play, "Yes! And
. . ." That will take them off their verbal agenda and will
provide them with an experience. They will see you as a person
rather than a sounding board and enter into an experience with
you.

**What do I do when interviewers say, "Tell me about
yourself"?**

They only say that when you are acting like a victim and are
waiting for a question or an instruction. You can avoid being
asked to tell about yourself at the beginning by telling your
first truth as soon as you sit down. In the middle of a meeting,
if the interviewer asks you to talk about yourself, and you
do, you are in trouble. The party is over because if you talk
about yourself you will create an isolating experience. The
interviewer will become an audience instead of a fellow player
in an experience. It is possible you were asked to tell about
yourself because neither of you was having an experience.
Whatever the reason, you should take it as a cue to develop
or extend the experience further. Go for a brand-new truth
line; play "Yes! And . . ." or Extend, Intensify and Enlarge.
Instead of telling them about yourself, show them! When you

show instead of tell, you provide an experience, and that will preclude the interviewer's need to be told who you are.

Won't it seem as if I'm avoiding talking about myself if I don't answer the question?

It depends on how you handle it. If you exhibit any desperation in talking about something other than yourself, it will seem like you're avoiding it. But if you have fun, the interviewer won't notice or won't care that you are not answering the question.

If I find myself in the middle of telling a story that is creating isolation, what should I do?

If the interviewer is just acting like an audience, finish your story immediately and get back on your interview focus. Ending the story earlier than usual can be the beginning of an experience between you. The new ending could be a springboard into something new. You might pause for a response and continue from there with a "Yes! And . . ." or you might tell another truth.

Since I'm supposed to avoid asking questions, how do I handle an instructional meeting?

I have been involved in large meetings designed specifically to provide information and answer actors' questions, and my experience is that if you have a specific question and can't find the answer elsewhere, ask it. What usually happens at these meetings, though, is that inauthentic actors use their questions as opportunities to have their face seen. "See me, remember me, and if my question is as brilliant as I think it is, you'll have to remember me." In fact, all they're doing is manipulating the auditors, the directors, casting directors, agents, or judges. And those actors will be remembered because no one likes to be manipulated. Those people know the game. They know what's going on. And they're going to react negatively to those actors.

What about the schmoozing that goes on before and after auditions? Should I approach it the same as interviews?

Yes, your interview work should come in handy during the periods of schmoozing that sometimes accompany auditions. However, there is another issue that should concern you. When you are auditioning, do you schmooze before or after the audition? If you have prepared your audition, and they start to schmooze you, you should say, from a position of equality, "I'm ready to read. Let's read and then we can chat afterward if you like." Be pleasant with no put-downs. They will say, "Great." Then you read, and at the end of your audition, they will either say, "Thank you. That was terrific. We will be in touch." Or they will say, "Sit down. Who are you? Where did you come from? I love you. Let's talk."

When they attempt to schmooze with you before the audition, they are only schmoozing to be polite. Veteran casting director Alice Cassidy offers: "Come in and say hello, and get comfortable in the room quickly. Telling one anecdote is okay, but three or four is way too much. I understand actors do that to control their nerves, but the people in the room have a million other things on their minds. They are in there to get the work done, not socialize."[6] When you respond the way I suggest, you make it easy for them because after they see you audition there may be no reason for you to spend more time together. Time is precious.

There is another reason to avoid schmoozing before an audition. You can avoid their telling you how to do the scene. If they do start to tell you how to play the scene, you should say, "Let me show you what I prepared and then if you want to make adjustments, great." They will be pleased to know you have prepared the scene. If you do a great reading, avoid schmoozing and get out of there! After a great reading, everything else is about losing the job.

Essentially, I recommend that you get in and out without schmoozing. It's the audition that counts. Whenever any schmoozing does occur, of course, you should use your new interviewing tools. It is simple common sense. June Lowry Johnson, a multiple Emmy award-winning casting director (*NYPD Blue*), says, "I am more touched by the people who just come in and do it and, after the reading ends, leave quickly, not lingering in the room. If you just do it and leave, you leave a much better impression. You leave them with what you just did and not with the awkward moments of hanging on."[7]

If I leave the audition without having a chat, how will they know I want the job? And how do I handle the time while I wait for them to call?

The fact that you showed up for the audition communicates that you want the job. However, it is important to your career and your health that you don't want the job, even though you do. It doesn't improve your chances of getting the job to go home wanting the job. Instead, you are anxious for the rest of the day or week until you hear. This can screw up everything else in your life. Be a professional. If you get the audition appointment, your attitude should be, "I'm pleased they want me to come in and read." That is very different from, "I am afraid. I have to go read. I want this job so badly. I could pay the rent. I could be a regular on a series. I could win an Oscar."

The only thing that can help you before an audition is to prepare for the audition as thoroughly as you can, to make choices, and to rehearse. After the audition you forget about it. The rest of your day will then be open for you to focus on your next order of business.

What if I need some information to help prepare the audition?

After you receive the sides, if there is information you need about the material, ask the casting director or staff. The time to get information is before you complete your preparation, not at the audition. Remember, if you haven't fully prepared, then all bets are off. Casting director Carol Lefko says, "Before you come in, do your homework to find out what the show is about. The casting director has no time to answer obvious questions about the show to fifty actors, when so many actors are in the waiting room. Ask your agent to help you. They'll know because there's sometimes a storyline given in the breakdowns. Other than that, ask the assistant to the casting director, or come in beforehand and read the script if it's available. And, finally, there is nothing like an actor who comes in with a genuine smile on his face, hands you his picture and résumé stapled together, and nails the audition."[8]

How important is thorough audition preparation?

Going in and winging an audition or telling the casting directors that you just got the sides and haven't had time to prepare will guarantee that you do not get called back. In addition, they will not like you, and your chances of being called in for future auditions will be diminished.

Here are some casting directors' responses:

Dan Shaner: "One thing that I have always *hated* is when an actor comes in and says, 'Okay, tell me what you want and I'll just do it.' This tells me that they have given no thought to the preparation and characterization. They basically are asking me to do their work. Other times they will say, 'I have made a couple of choices but don't know which way to go.' Well, go ahead and show me what you have prepared and then we'll talk about it."[9]

John Levey: "Don't be unprepared and don't blame me for you[r] being unprepared. People come in and say, 'Oh, I just got these sides,' and I'd like to *kill* them because I made the sides available at least the day before."[10]

Dean Fronk: "If you are coming in for a feature and you haven't taken the time to read the script, you're nowhere near as prepared as the actor who has."[11]

Barbara Claman: "You'd better memorize it. Know your lines, come in, and hold your script in your hands, so that if you forget your lines, you can look down. Actors can pick up a script the day before and have the time overnight to study it. That's not cold reading. If you haven't memorized it, if you don't have it in your insides, then you haven't crafted that scene. How are you going to get the job?"[12]

Lori Cobe: "You need to prepare and be prepared before you audition, or it's just going to be 'Thank you' and on to the next person. You get one shot per role and usually you get only a few minutes to make an impression."[13]

Not getting the sides early enough to memorize and prepare thoroughly is frequently the victim's excuse for not doing the work. My student, William Schallert, adds:

"When I was president of the guild [SAG] in 1980, one of the things we accomplished was to provide that a full script must be available for every actor who is going to audition. They don't have to send it to you, but they have to provide you with it if you go to where they are, so long as they've got it. If they say, 'All we have is sides,' and you see pages fifty-two, fifty-three, fifty-four, and pages eighteen and nineteen, you say, 'Where did these come from? You have a script and I am entitled to the script.' Demand it and don't worry about it. It is your right as a professional actor. Once you have seen the whole script, it will give you a much better fix about what the sides are about. 'Sides' is a misnomer anyway. Sides are from the theater and are a different thing entirely. They call them sides but they aren't. It is just a way of demeaning you and making you more of a victim. You are entitled."[14]

If the casting director asks how I like working with my agent, how do I handle that?

If you do not know if the casting director has a relationship with your agent, it is best to assume that they do. Share anything you appreciate about your agent. If you are not fond of your agent or what he or she isn't doing for you, do not share that. Blaming others for your lack of success is not attractive. You are encouraged not to lie, so a joke may be in order. Your response might be, "When I'm working, I love him. When I'm not, I hate him," or "I like her ten percent more than a total stranger."

If the casting director asks how old I am and I don't want to tell, how do I handle that?

If you are successful in creating an experience with the interviewers, there won't be an opportunity for them to ask you that question. However, suppose they do ask the question and you have previously decided that you don't wish to reveal your age. I know of two approaches to this issue. First, you can create an authentic experience around not telling them by playing with them. For instance, let's say that I am the actor, and you ask me how old I am:

Casting Director: How old are you?

Book: Can you keep a secret?

Casting Director: Sure.

Book: So can I.

Here is another example of playing:

Casting Director: How old are you?

Book: Oh, old enough that I don't have a curfew.

Still another example:

Casting Director: How old are you?

Book: I am over twenty-one. Why, do you want me to buy beer?

In these examples, you play with the issue while communicating that you are not going to tell him or her. And you do it in a fashion that doesn't make you appear to be arrogant. The second approach is a direct one. Tell the director that you do not reveal your age. "I never reveal my age." This works better if you have actually been advised not to reveal your age because then you can add, "My agent told me not to tell my age to anyone." With this approach you authentically tell the director that you are not going to reveal your age. The casting director is not going to assume that he or she has more creditability than your agent or manager.

What if the casting director becomes persistent about knowing my age?

The reason for the persistence is that you have been inauthentic in answering the original question. Your answer came from a victim stance or from your manipulating the situation. If you had put your answer out there authentically, he or she would have stopped asking.

Why wouldn't I want to tell a casting director my age?

This is the kind of thing that you want to discuss with your representatives. For instance, suppose you play sixteen to twenty and you are actually thirty-four years old. You might be limiting yourself by telling your age. I don't think actors should ever limit themselves. You avoid the self-limitation and you avoid lying by handling the situation with the approaches I have suggested.

How about answering the age question by telling my age range?

The agent or casting director is a professional and sees what your age range is. Many actors extend their age range beyond reason. It is also frustrating and annoying when you do not answer the question when they asked, "How old are you?" Instead, you answer another question you would have preferred they asked, "What age range do you play?"

How do I handle an unscrupulous casting director or agent who wants sexual favors from me?

All bets are off. Get out of there.

What if I've done all the exercises and I'm still feeling like a victim?

Should you, after doing the exercises and practice interviews in this book, find that you have no success in shaking off your victim stance, try one more exercise: do the Attitude Line—I Am exercise from Chapter 5. However, change the attitude line from "I am" to "I'm a victim." After fully taking on that attitude line, do a practice interview and stay on the focus, retaining that attitude, "I'm a victim." After this interview you should have a new sense of your victim stance and will probably decide that enough is enough. Further, this full-body identification with your victim stance will increase your self-awareness of any aspects of your victim stance.

If I am consciously employing my new interview technique in order to get what I want, aren't I practicing manipulation?

Manipulation is a process devoid of spontaneity and authenticity. It is initiated by your defense system and is frequently a result of your being unconscious or lacking self-awareness. Your new interview technique—a collection of tools to heighten the presentation of your authentic self—is grounded in spontaneity, authenticity, consciousness and self-awareness. Martha Graham said, "The aim of technique is to free the spirit."

Conclusion

If you compare the first and last interviews of the four actors we have tracked, you should be able to answer the following questions with positive answers.

Have they improved their chances of being called back for auditions?

Are they more likely to be signed by agents and managers?

Is a producer more likely to think they will bring something special to his or her project?

Do you think their batting averages have improved?

If you read this book without doing the exercises, you will probably find that your interviews have improved, but have they improved sufficiently? Performance improves with experience, and doing the exercises provides that experience. I have designed the exercises to lead you through the challenges sequentially. The sequence itself has been designed to facilitate learning by leading you through the challenges from less to more difficult. Doing the exercises and improvisations with a friend will provide you with practice where there is nothing at stake, except your learning and growth. You will then be able to handle the pressures of real interviews. Nothing is learned that isn't experienced, including these words.

Notes

Introduction

1.   Stephen Book, *Book on Acting: Improvisation Technique for the Professional Actor in Film, Theater & Television* (Los Angeles: Silman-James Press, 2002).

1. How Do You Present Yourself?

1.   Karen Kondazian, "Sculpting Your Career," *Drama-Logue*, 8/25/94.
2.   Jack Lee Rosenberg and Beverly Kitaen-Morse, *The Intimate Couple* (Atlanta: Turner Publishing, 1996), p. 175.
3.   Karen Kondazian, "Sculpting Your Career," *Drama-Logue*, 9/26/96.
4.   Karen Kondazian, "The Actor's Way," *Back Stage West*, 12/4/97.
5.   Hettie Lynne Hurtes, "Beyond Talent: What Casting Directors Want from Your Audition," *Back Stage West*, 10/29/93.

3. Building an Experience

1.   Stephen Book, *Book on Acting: Improvisation Technique for the Professional Actor in Film, Theater & Television*, p. 489.
2.   Evolved from Viola Spolin, "Mirror Exercise," *Improvisation for the Theater*. (Evanston, IL: Northwestern University Press, 1963), p. 60.
3.   Evolved from Stephen Book, "Reflection Listening," *Book on Acting: Improvisation Technique for the Professional Actor in Film, Theater & Television*, p. 206. Also evolved from Viola Spolin, "Mirror Speech," *Theater Game File* (St. Louis: Cemrel, Inc., 1975), p. A52.

4. Heightening the Experience

1.   Jack Lee Rosenberg and Beverly Kitaen-Morse, *The Intimate Couple*, p. 45.
2.   Stephen Book, *Book on Acting: Improvisation Technique for the Professional Actor in Film, Theater & Television*, p. 330. Also evolved from Viola Spolin, "Explore and Heighten (Transformation of Beat)," *Improvisation for the Theater*, p. 235, and Viola Spolin, "Explore and Heighten," *Theater Game File*, p. C6.
3.   Behnoosh Khalili, "How Do You Get an Agent?" *Back Stage West*, 11/25/99.
4.   Karen Kondazian, "The Actor's Way," *Back Stage West*, 12/4/97.
5.   Neil Gordon, *Sacrifice of Isaac*. New York: Random House, 1995.

5. Tracking and Changing Behavior

1.   Evolved from Viola Spolin, "Score," *Theater Games for the Lone Actor* (Evanston, IL: Northwestern University Press, 2001), p. 115.
2.   Evolved from Stephen Book, "Attitude Lines," *Book on Acting: Improvisation Technique for the Professional Actor in Film, Theater &*

Television, p. 274. Also evolved from "Hold It! A" in Viola Spolin, *Improvisation for the Theater*, p. 259, and "Hold It! #1" in Viola Spolin, *Theater Game File*, p. C27.

6. Creating Your Program

1. Jack Lee Rosenberg and Beverly Kitaen-Morse, *The Intimate Couple*, p. 50.

7. Boundaries

1. Jack Lee Rosenberg with Marjorie L. Rand and Diane Asay, *Body, Self, & Soul.* (Atlanta: Humanics Limited, 1985), p. 319.
2. Evolved from a Viola Spolin exercise, that's untitled and unpublished.
3. Evolved from a Rosenberg-Kitaen Integrative Body Pschotherapy exercise, that's untitled and unpublished.
4. Jay Michael Beeber, "The 12 Commandments of Auditions," *Back Stage West*, 11/11/99.

8. The Witness

1. Evolved from Viola Spolin, "No Motion," *Improvisation for the Theater*, p. 189, and Viola Spolin, "No Motion Warm-Up" and "Walking," *Theater Game File*, pp. A30, A31.

9. It's Your Career

1. Karen Kondazian, "Sculpting Your Career," *Drama-Logue*, 9/21/95.
2. Jackie Apodaca, "The Working Actor," *Back Stage West*, 9/1/05.
3. Hettie Lynne Hurtes, "Beyond Talent: What Casting Directors Want from Your Audition," *Back Stage West*, 10/29/93.
4. Jackie Apodaca, "The Working Actor," *Back Stage West*, 9/1/05.
5. Jackie Apodaca, "The Working Actor," *Back Stage West*, 9/1/05.
6. Karen Kondazian, "Sculpting Your Career," *Drama-Logue*, 10/10/96.
7. Karen Kondazian, "Sculpting Your Career," *Drama-Logue*, 9/7/95.
8. Karen Kondazian, "Sculpting Your Career," *Drama-Logue*, 5/16/96.
9. Karen Kondazian, op. cit., 9/26/96.
10. Karen Kondazian, op. cit.,12/4/97.
11. Jay Michael Beeber, "The 12 Commandments of Auditions," *Back Stage West*, 11/11/99.
12. Karen Kondazian, "Sculpting Your Career," *Drama-Logue*, 2/9/95.
13. Elias Stimac, "Lori Cobe: Non-Stop Casting Director," *Drama-Logue*, 8/8/91.
14. Stephen Book, *Book on Acting: Improvisation Technique for the Professional Actor in Film, Theater & Television*, p. 324.

Acknowledgements

Many thanks to: the late Viola Spolin for opening my eyes to the worlds of education, spontaneity, and improvisation; Jack Rosenberg and Beverly Kitaen-Morse for their work in character styles, authenticity, and journal-writing; Darlene Basch for vetting specific passages on psychology; my workshop assistant, Elizabeth Dement, for her help in the early stages of the Interview Project and for teaching it at my workshop using the first-draft manuscript of this book; Dorothy and Leo Braudy for being there; Adam Ferrara, who keeps me laughing; Gwen Feldman at Silman-James Press for suggesting a second book; Marjorie Hanlon, editor; Laurie Fitzpatrick for her authenticity, creativity, beauty, individuality, and friendship.

Special thanks to the following actors for participating in the Interview Project and making their own unique contributions:

Michael Adler, Heidi Ahn, Linda Aigner, Jenine Anderson, Amanda Anka, Laura Aryeh, Michelle Ashlee, Heather Ashton, Scott Atkinson, Brendan Aucoin, Susanne Averitt, Betsy Baldwin, Martina Barrett, Ed Bell, Judith Marie Bergan, Melina Bielefelt, Greg Bierne, Greg Binkley, Pierson Blaetz, Nancy Blier, Susanna Blinkoff, David Boreanaz, John Bower, Lou Briggs, Haynes Brooke, Rebecca Brooks, Veronica Brown, Mark Burton, Al Caramatti, Stephanie Cameron, Andrew Casagrande, Lisa Casandra, Dan Castle, Ben Caswell, Suzanne Celeste, Cathleen Chin, Charles Chun, Mercedes Colon, Shanna Corrine, Suzette Craft, Kat Cressida, Robin Curtis, Al D'Andrea, Lauren Daniels, Kathleen Darcy, Liz Dean, Athena Demos, Robert Dorfman, Larry Drake, Bill Dwyer, Adrienne Ellis, Alex Endeshaw, Pamela Evans, Shannon Everitt, Susan Fallender, Erik Fallin, Adam Ferrara, Barbara Ferris, Rob Roy Fitzgerald, Alana Flanagan, Dorian Frankel, Gibson Frazier, Paul Friedman, Debbie Fuhrman, Mark Fuller, Garvin Funches, Graham Gathright, Brian Gattas, Dan Gauthier, Diana Georger, Morgan Gillio, Jody Gottschalk, Meta Golding, Lisa Gould, Ashley Graham, Javier Grajeda, Kerri Green, Kim Mai

Guest, Dan Gunther, Illya Haase, Aaron Haedt, Todd Hanson, Jane Harnick, Alan Heitz, Kei Higashi, Arabella Holzbog, Olivia Honegger, Mary Ellen Hooper, Lori Horrowitz, Chase Hoyt, Paul Hughs, Leslie Hyland, Aaron Isbecki, Krish Iyer, DeAnn Jeffries, Gunther Jenson, Brian Jett, Georja Jones, Renee Jones, Reef Karim, Brixton Karnes, Johnny Kastle, Elizabeth Kate, Nancy Katera, Helen Keany, Colom Keating, Terri Kempner, Beth Kennedy, Jennifer Kingsley, Aaron Kjenas, Dufflyn Lammers, Michael Leavy, Art LeFleur, Nathan LeGrand, Janna Levenstein, Karen Lew, Toni Lewis, Sarah Long, Giselle Loren, Lara Lyon, Christina Ma, Jacey Margolis, Joe Marino, Andrew Marks, Brenda Mathews, Cathy McAllister, Ken McCandles, Douglas McDonald, Lex Medlin, Daniel Lynch Miller, Pam Monakee, Michael Monks, David Morgan, Talbert Morton, Denise Moses, Sandy Moy, Gary Murphy, Marcia Nanetti, Karen Nation, Shaye Nelson, Michael Ness, Ingo Neuhaus, Steve Niel, Montana Nolte, Carolyn O'Brien, Karyn O'Bryant, Sean Ogren, Ken Palmer, Claire Partin, Tina Patrick, Jon Pennell, Scott Perry, Thomas Pescod, Tracy Phillips, Linda Pierce, Alan Piper, Margaret Reed, Nikko Rey, Mindi Rickles, Jack Riley, Beth Robbins, Elise Robbins, Gregory Jou-Jon Roche, Eric Roth, Richard Rothenberg, Darby Rowe, Akemi Royer, John Rubinow, Andrea Ruth, William Schallert, Stu Schreiber, Erica Segal, Susan Segal, Naomi Serotoff, Charles Shaugnessy, Danica Sheridan, Patricia Sill, Gabrielle Sinclair, Emily Mura Smith, Paige Scurti Sternin, Nell Stewart, Laura Stockman, Wisconsin Sturm, Nancy Sullivan, Tom Sunstrom, Jay Taylor, Louisa Taylor, Eric "ET" Tecosky, Meredith Louise Thomas, Shelley Thorenson, Scott Thun, Christopher Titus, Marilyn Tokuda, Melissa Trueblood, Mung Ling Tsui, Mark Valley, Marnie Valley, Tony Vasek, Leah Verrill, Harry Victor, Abby Vinson, Jimmy Vollman, Ian Wallach, Vincent Ward, Malcolm-Jamal Warner, Krista Weidig, Tegan West, Eileen Westenberg, Daisy White, Karen White, Canon Wing, Maia Winters, John Worful, Karl Wright, Andrew Wynn, Art Ybarra, Estera Zarko, Christopher Zawalski, Dawn Zummo.

Praise for Stephen Book and Improvisation Technique

*I commend Stephen Book's work and highly recommend him to the
theater community.*

—Viola Spolin

*A very intelligent and highly skilled teacher of acting. Actors find him
exciting to work with and get a great deal from his particular form of
teaching.*

—John Houseman

*I have watched the class at work, numerous times, and have been
intrigued and impressed with Mr. Book's special abilities, and with the
progress immediately observable. I find his work most valuable.*

—Alan Schneider

*In adapting improvisation exercises to script work, Stephen Book
challenges some of the received wisdom of modern American training
and offers a practical method for professional actors who want to
learn how to infuse their work with spontaneity. Book's excercises
demonstrate how much farther you can go, imaginatively speaking,
when acting.*

—Back Stage West

*I was a student in Stephen Book's acting class during the three or so
years he was writing this book, so I have experienced its riches first-
hand. I know how much I gained, and I witnessed the growth of the
other actors in the class. I still remember our first round of scene work
and the remarkable transformation of each actor's work after we did
the First-Level Improvisations. It was a startling demonstration of the
transforming power of the Improvisation Technique we were learning.
And the best was yet to come. I was seventy-five when I began the class,
a professional actor for fifty years. I finished not long after I turned
seventy-nine, my craft immeasurably enriched and strengthened, with
access to emotional resources I did not realize I had within me. As I get
ready to start rehearsals for a new play, I have a fresh sense of myself
in the work I have been doing my whole professional life. Priceless!*

—William Schallert, President, Screen Actors Guild (1979-81)

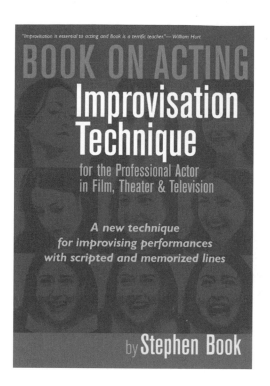

Improvisation is essential to acting and Book is a terrific teacher.

—William Hurt

Coming as I did from stand-up comedy—and with a movie part in hand—I was greatly in need of a teacher and a system that could bring out and begin to develop my natural skills in a short time. Stephen Book and his workshop were just such a combination. I continue working with him to my great benefit.

—George Carlin

Stephen Book is a genius! I took his Improvisation Technique class and have had several private-coaching sessions with him. I immediately saw vast improvement in my stage and film work. His technique is the perfect addition to my traditional theater training. I am thrilled to have a new toolbox for creating a character.

—Sanaa Lathan